D0592391

Especially for

_____

From

_____

Date

_____

© 2011 by Barbour Publishing, Inc.

ISBN 978-1-61626-159-7

Compiled by Joanie Garborg.

All quotes and scriptures are taken from *Daily Wisdom for Women*
by Carol L. Fitzpatrick, published by Barbour Publishing, Inc. Some
quotes have been edited slightly to help them stand alone.

All rights reserved. No part of this publication may be reproduced or
transmitted for commercial purposes, except for brief quotations in
printed reviews, without written permission of the publisher.

Scripture quotations, unless otherwise noted, are taken from the
New American Standard Bible, © 1960, 1962, 1963, 1968, 1971,
1972, 1973, 1975, 1977, 1995 by The Lockman Foundation. Used by
permission.

Scripture quotations marked NIV are taken from the HOLY BIBLE,
NEW INTERNATIONAL VERSION®. NIV®. Copyright © 1973,
1978, 1984 by International Bible Society. Used by permission of
Zondervan. All rights reserved.

Published by Barbour Publishing, Inc., P.O. Box 719, Uhrichsville,
Ohio 44683, www.barbourbooks.com

*Our mission is to publish and distribute inspirational products offering
exceptional value and biblical encouragement to the masses.*

Member of the
Evangelical Christian
Publishers Association

Printed in China.

Wisdom for Women

inspiration for every day!

BARBOUR
PUBLISHING

In His Image

So God created man in his own image, in the image of God he created him; male and female he created them.

Genesis 1:27 NIV

A whole new year stretches out before you, like a crisp carpet of newly fallen snow. What kind of footprints will you leave? Maybe your strides will be gigantic leaps of faith. Or perhaps you will take tiny steps of slow, steady progress. Some imprints might even be creative expressions, woman-sized angels in the snow.

Garden of Prayer

When the woman saw that the tree was good for food,
and that it was a delight to the eyes,
and that the tree was desirable to make one wise,
she took from its fruit and ate.

Genesis 3:6

Two thousand years later, Jesus returned to
another garden as His place of prayer. And on the
cross the sacrifice of His life provided forgiveness,
once again allowing access to God's presence. . .
now within a spiritual garden of prayer.

A Wise Woman

To receive instruction in wise behavior, righteousness, justice and equity; to give prudence to the naive, to the youth knowledge and discretion, a wise man will hear and increase in learning, and a man of understanding will acquire wise counsel, to understand a proverb and a figure, the words of the wise and their riddles.

Proverbs 1:3–6

Lord, surround me with friends who know You and Your Word. Surround me in a crisis so I can still hear Your voice of wisdom and reason.

God of Covenants

I have set my rainbow in the clouds, and it will be the sign of the covenant between me and the earth.

Genesis 9:13 NIV

Every day God freely displays His blessings. Are we too busy or disinterested to appreciate their wonder? Even if we've forgotten He's there, reminders are all around, for He is the God of covenants. In a world where promises (or covenants) are disregarded routinely, I need God's kind of stability.

"Follow Me"

*"Come, follow me," Jesus said, "and
I will make you fishers of men."*
Matthew 4:19 NIV

Jesus came not only to save but to teach men and
women how to have true servants' hearts. The
substance of ministry is service. When the apostles
agreed to follow Christ, they accepted the call on
His terms, not theirs.

Start Each Day with God

In the morning, O LORD, you hear my voice;
in the morning I lay my requests before you
and wait in expectation.
Psalm 5:3 NIV

Lord, I wander around like those who have no hope, forgetting to ask You for wise solutions to my dilemmas. Help me remember to come to You before I start my day.

Surrender All

*I will bless her and will surely give you a son by her.
I will bless her so that she will be the mother of nations;
kings of peoples will come from her.*

Genesis 17:16 NIV

Lord, only You have the power to override earthly
impossibilities. I pray today that no matter what
appears to be impossible in my life, I'll be able to
surrender it to Your care and trust.

From the Heart

And when you are praying, do not use meaningless repetition as the Gentiles do, for they suppose that they will be heard for their many words.

Matthew 6:7

Your prayers certainly don't have to be elaborate or polished. God does not judge your way with words. He knows your heart. He wants to hear from you. His Word says that your prayers rise up to heaven like incense from the earth. Remember to send a sweet savor His way daily.

Gift of Wisdom

For the LORD gives wisdom;
from His mouth come knowledge and understanding.
He stores up sound wisdom for the upright;
He is a shield to those who walk in integrity.

Proverbs 2:6–8

God's Word says wisdom is truly a gift since it comes from the mouth of God, from the very words He speaks. Know that if you hold fast to the precepts contained in the Bible, you will walk in integrity.

Set Free

And the LORD said,
"The outcry of Sodom and Gomorrah is indeed great,
and their sin is exceedingly grave."
Genesis 18:20

Lord, if I know someone caught in the deadly snare of sin, please remind me to pray for her. Only through You and Your Word can she be truly set free.

Born Again

For the gate is small and the way is narrow that leads to life, and there are few who find it.

Matthew 7:14

Knowing the right answers and then taking them to heart is critical in our spiritual life. You can't get to heaven unless you are truly born again. Lord, give me Your light that I may respond.

His Voice

Beware of the false prophets, who come to you in sheep's clothing, but inwardly are ravenous wolves. You will know them by their fruits.

Matthew 7:15–16

Those who abide in Christ preach the message that is consistent with the one Christ Himself taught. Lord, there are so many voices. Please help us to hear Yours, so that we won't be led astray.

The Power of God's Word

And when He got into the boat, His disciples followed
Him. And behold, there arose a great storm in the sea,
so that the boat was covered with the waves;
but Jesus Himself was asleep.

Matthew 8:23–24

Jesus took the disciples to the height of the storm's
raging fury, yet all the time He was with them.
Yes, the storms of life will attempt to ravage me,
but Christ is there, amid the frenzy, ready to
deliver by just the power of His Word.

The Lord Shall Reign Forever

The LORD is King forever and ever;
nations have perished from His land.
Psalm 10:16

God's Son, Jesus Christ, lives forever within those who call upon His name. And despite the efforts of the evil one, Jesus will remain King and will one day soon come back to claim this earth for His own, forever and ever.

Eternity?

*Upon the wicked He will rain snares; fire and
brimstone and burning wind will be the portion of their
cup. For the LORD is righteous; He loves righteousness;
the upright will behold His face.*

Psalm 11:6–7

To those who choose to obliterate from their
minds any notion of a "real hell," God says it *does*
exist. The flip side of hell, of course, is heaven,
the place where the righteous will behold His face.
Where will you choose to spend eternity?

Incredible Joy

*Help, L*ORD*, for the godly man ceases to be, for the
faithful disappear from among the sons of men.*
Psalm 12:1

Lord, I have watched people carry burdens that
humanly speaking should be unbearable. Yet with
these trials You give them incredible joy. I praise
You for all You are!

Change My Heart, Lord

The people who walk in darkness will see a great light;
those who live in a dark land,
the light will shine on them.

Isaiah 9:2

Lord, change the desire of my heart to seek and
know You better. Take my life and use me for
Your purposes.

So Precious

Therefore everyone who confesses Me before men, I will also confess him before My Father who is in heaven.
Matthew 10:32

If we know Jesus Christ and have responded to His invitation to receive Him as Savior, Jesus remains forever our advocate before the Father, saying with love, "She's mine." Know that you are so precious to Jesus that He gave His life for you. Doesn't it feel incredible to have Jesus as your defender?

Strength to Overcome

*Now Joseph was well-built and handsome, and after a
while his master's wife took notice of Joseph and said,
"Come to bed with me!" But he refused.*

Genesis 39:6–8 NIV

Lord, I can't look ahead to see how a critical
moment of obedience fits into Your overall plan.
Please give me Your strength when my human
desires threaten to overpower me.

The Hand of Faith

And the disciples came and said to Him,
"Why do You speak to them in parables?"
Matthew 13:10

He spoke in parables, or words of truth hidden
under an imaginary net. Only with the hand of
faith could these followers lift a corner of the net
and view the truth. Yet to those whom He knew
would respond, He provided plain words. How
open have you been to God's Word?

Family of Believers

*He came to His hometown and began teaching them
in their synagogue, so that they were astonished,
and said, "Where did this man get this wisdom
and these miraculous powers?"*

Matthew 13:54

Jesus came from God, full of wisdom. Those who
stood with Him during His earthly ministry had
true wisdom and understanding from God. They
made up His true family of believers. Lord, even if
my earthly family rejects me, You have promised to
be there for me.

In God's Hands

He reached down from on high and took hold of me;
he drew me out of deep waters.
He rescued me from my powerful enemy,
from my foes, who were too strong for me.

Psalm 18:16–17 NIV

The very nature and character of God demands that He rescue those whom He loves. He reaches out to us with His mighty hand of rescue. When confronted with a crisis, like David, you can put your life in His hands.

God Fulfills His Promises

*"I am God, the God of your father," he said.
"Do not be afraid to go down to Egypt, for I will make
you into a great nation there. I will go down to Egypt
with you, and I will surely bring you back again."*

Genesis 46:3–4 NIV

Lord, You are a God who fulfills promises.
I praise You!

Brilliant Forgiveness

And he said, "I am your brother Joseph, whom you sold into Egypt. Now do not be grieved or angry with yourselves, because you sold me here, for God sent me before you to preserve life."

Genesis 45:4–5

Lord, show me the brilliance of Your forgiveness that I might trust You in the trial and not miss the outcome You've planned.

Expanding Faith

*How is it that you do not understand that I did not
speak to you concerning bread? But beware of the
leaven of the Pharisees and Sadducees.*

Matthew 16:11

Jesus used a physical reality to get across a spiritual
truth. But the disciples missed the point. His
warning concerned the teaching of their religious
leaders, men who knew the scriptures and yet
denied Jesus as the Messiah. Lord, please expand
the little faith I have and provide me with real
comprehension.

"I Am"

The man said, "Who made you ruler and judge over us? Are you thinking of killing me as you killed the Egyptian?" Then Moses was afraid and thought, "What I did must have become known."

Exodus 2:14 NIV

Moses felt unworthy to serve God because of his great sin. But instead of rebuke, Moses hears, "I will be with you. . .I am who I am" (Exodus 3:12–14 NIV). This is the same "I Am" who calls you to serve Him today.

"Who Do You Say I Am?"

"But what about you?" he asked. "Who do you say
I am?" Simon Peter answered, "You are the Christ,
the Son of the living God."
Matthew 16:15–16 NIV

Jesus repeatedly asked this question to those
who followed after Him. He knew that in a short
while He would be gone, and all these fledgling
Christians would have to bolster their faith with
His words and actions. Jesus wanted to be sure they
would not allow the world's viewpoint to diminish
who He was.

Where Are You Today?

My God, my God, why have You forsaken me?
Far from my deliverance are the words of my groaning.

Psalm 22:1

Where are you today? On the road, walking toward
Him? Sitting down, too bewildered to even
formulate questions? Or are you kneeling right
at His bleeding feet?

All Our Needs

*Then Moses said to the LORD, "Please, Lord,
I have never been eloquent, neither recently nor in time
past, nor since You have spoken to Your servant;
for I am slow of speech and slow of tongue."*

Exodus 4:10

The Lord wanted Moses to understand that He
could and would meet all of his needs. Instead,
Moses settled for allowing Aaron to speak for him.
Do you give the Lord part of your problem and
then halfway through start solving it yourself?

Give Me Strength, Lord

Then Pharaoh sent for Moses and Aaron,
and said to them, "I have sinned this time;
the LORD is the righteous one, and I
and my people are the wicked ones."

Exodus 9:27

Lord, it's so easy to see Pharaoh's obstinate streak.
Give me strength to admit when I'm wrong. Give
me strength to come to You in repentance.

Keep Me Faithful

*Then Peter said to Him, "Behold, we have
left everything and followed You;
what then will there be for us?"*

Matthew 19:27

Lord, I can't even imagine what You have in store
for me in heaven. Please keep me faithful to
complete the duties You've called me to on earth.

Stand Firm

A scoundrel and villain, who goes about with a corrupt mouth, who winks with his eye, signals with his feet and motions with his fingers, who plots evil with deceit in his heart—he always stirs up dissension.

Proverbs 6:12–14 NIV

Lord, all around me are those who seek to divert the path of my life. Help me to stand firmly on Your unchanging Word. Help me to trust You, the Ancient of Days, who always remains the same.

The Promised Messiah

Slay the Passover lamb. You shall take a bunch of hyssop and dip it in the blood which is in the basin, and apply some of the blood that is in the basin to the lintel and the two doorposts; and none of you shall go outside the door of his house until morning.

Exodus 12:21–22

Lord Jesus Christ, I thank You for being my promised Messiah and Passover Lamb. I thank You for Your sacrifice so that my sins could be forgiven.

Day 34

In Obedience

*The LORD was going before them in a pillar
of cloud by day to lead them on the way,
and in a pillar of fire by night to give them light,
that they might travel by day and by night.
He did not take away the pillar of cloud by day,
nor the pillar of fire by night, from before the people.*

Exodus 13:21–22

Lord, let me not forget that I have seen Your
power. Help me to continue walking in obedience
to You.

The Invitation

The kingdom of heaven may be compared to a king who gave a wedding feast for his son. And he sent out his slaves to call those who had been invited to the wedding feast, and they were unwilling to come.

Matthew 22:2–3

When God sent His Son to earth, He invited all men and women to a wedding feast. Lord, You've invited me to dine with You. Let me graciously accept Your righteousness as the "wedding clothes" You provide.

Remember the Sabbath

Remember the sabbath day, to keep it holy.
Six days you shall labor and do all your work,
but the seventh day is a sabbath of the LORD your
God; in it you shall not do any work.

Exodus 20:8–10

In the very beginning of our marriage my husband
and I made a decision to honor God on Sunday.
He has blessed us for this faithful commitment,
providing weekly spiritual guidance and also giving
our bodies and souls the rest they require.

Mourning to Dancing

You have turned for me my mourning into dancing;
You have loosed my sackcloth and girded
me with gladness.
Psalm 30:11

At one time, there were many people whom I felt incapable of pardoning. God's name topped the list. But I finally surrendered my life to Christ. And God's power of forgiveness has turned my own mourning into dancing.

A Choice

Does not wisdom call, and understanding lift up her
voice? On top of the heights beside the way, where
the paths meet, she takes her stand. . . . For wisdom
is better than jewels; and all desirable things cannot
compare with her.

Proverbs 8:1–2, 11

Notice in this passage that wisdom is a choice.
We can walk right past it. Wisdom is at the very
precipice of every decision. Lord, You lay before
me a path of righteousness. Help me desire to walk
with You!

A Glimpse of Heaven

You shall make holy garments for Aaron your brother,
for glory and for beauty. . .that he may
minister as priest to Me.
Exodus 28:2, 4

Notice that the priests were appointed by God to
minister directly to Him. God didn't want them
to forget whom they served. Lord, Your Majesty
is incredible. I know that the things of beauty on
earth are but a glimpse of all that's in heaven.

Still Forgiven

*Then Jesus said to them, "You will all fall away because
of Me this night."... But Peter said to Him,
"Even though all may fall away because of You,
I will never fall away."*

Matthew 26:31–33

Later that night, Peter would know without any
doubt that Jesus had tried to warn him. Then he
would look into those intense eyes and understand
that because Christ went to Calvary, even this sin
of denial could be forgiven.

Aren't You Glad?

When He set for the sea its boundary so that
the water would not transgress His command,
when He marked out the foundations of the earth;
then I was beside Him, as a master workman.

Proverbs 8:29–30

Somehow we have turned around history. Humans are
not in charge. God is. And He's still commanding
the dawn to happen and the earth to keep spinning
and the stars to remain in the sky. Aren't you glad?

Willing to Serve

*Then the whole Israelite community withdrew
from Moses' presence, and everyone who was willing
and whose heart moved him came and brought an
offering to the LORD for the work on the
Tent of Meeting, for all its service.*

Exodus 35:20–21 NIV

Lord, You've created within me something to be
used to further Your kingdom. Please enable me
to open my hands willingly in service.

True Sorrow

*They spat on Him, and took the reed and began to
beat Him on the head. After they had mocked Him,
they took the scarlet robe off Him and put
His own garments back on Him,
and led Him away to crucify Him.*
Matthew 27:30–31

Lord, You sacrificed all You had to provide my
eternal salvation. Help me today to express true
sorrow for my sins.

The Perfect Sacrifice

*Jesus came from Nazareth in Galilee and was baptized
by John in the Jordan. Immediately coming up
out of the water, He saw the heavens opening,
and the Spirit like a dove descending upon Him;
and a voice came out of the heavens: "You are My
beloved Son, in You I am well-pleased."*

Mark 1:9–11

Father, the picture can't be any clearer. Jesus is
Your Son and You are pleased with His perfect life
and His perfect sacrifice for my sins.

A Living Sacrifice

*Then the LORD called to Moses and spoke to him
from the tent of meeting, saying,
"Speak to the sons of Israel and say to them,
'When any man of you brings an offering to the LORD,
you shall bring your offering of animals
from the herd or the flock.'"*

Leviticus 1:1–2

Lord, how grateful I am for Jesus, Your
unblemished Lamb. Might I willingly become a
living sacrifice through service to You as I take the
gospel to this needy world.

Every Need

*Now Simon's mother-in-law was lying sick with a fever;
and immediately they spoke to Jesus about her.
And He came to her and raised her up, taking her by the
hand, and the fever left her, and she waited on them.*

Mark 1:30–31

Jesus meets every need for every situation if
we come to Him in faith. Lord, thank You for
always going well beyond what I expect or ask.
I appreciate Your attention to priorities.

Guide Me, Lord

The woman of folly is boisterous, she is naive and knows nothing. She sits at the doorway of her house, on a seat by the high places of the city, calling to those who pass by, who are making their paths straight: "Whoever is naive, let him turn in here," and to him who lacks understanding she says, "Stolen water is sweet; and bread eaten in secret is pleasant."

Proverbs 9:13–18

Lord, please guide me to the place You envision for me.

Dare to Make a Difference

"Who are My mother and My brothers?
For whoever does the will of God,
he is My brother and sister and mother."
Mark 3:33, 35

As women, are we using our precious moments
to further the gospel, or are we involved in trivial
pursuits? Do we stand alongside those in our
families who dare to make a difference? Or have
we added to their burdens by missing their obvious
purpose?

The Power to Heal

*A woman who had had a hemorrhage for twelve years
. . .after hearing about Jesus, she came up in the crowd
behind Him and touched His cloak. For she thought,
"If I just touch His garments, I will get well."*
Mark 5:25, 27–28

Lord, You heal me when I come to You, by
renewing my spirit and deepening my faith.
I worship Your majesty and power.

The Call to Obedience

Speak to the sons of Israel, saying,
"These are the creatures which you may eat from
all the animals that are on the earth."
Leviticus 11:2

Lord, Your call to obedience may not always make sense to me, but help me remember that You have a reason.

Fearfully and Wonderfully Made

*For You formed my inward parts; You wove me in my
mother's womb. I will give thanks to You, for I am
fearfully and wonderfully made; wonderful are Your
works, and my soul knows it very well.*

Psalm 139:13–14

God rejoiced at your birth. You were fashioned
exactly the way He wanted you. How incredible to
comprehend that when you awake in the morning,
God is already thinking about you!

For the Future

*LORD, make me to know my end and what is the extent
of my days; let me know how transient I am.*

Psalm 39:4

God wants us to trust Him for our future. To know
our lifespan would affect us every day of our life.
So, God has guarded this secret as a great favor to
us. To worry about the future is to be uncertain of
your eternity.

The Wise Heart

*The wise of heart will receive commands,
but a babbling fool will be ruined. He who
walks in integrity walks securely, but he who
perverts his ways will be found out.*

Proverbs 10:8–9

Lord, help us to stress honesty and obedience to
the truth of Your Word, and to shower our kids
with unconditional love so that our children can
grow to maturity in a secure emotional place.

Jesus' Touch

Jesus left that place and went to the vicinity of Tyre. . . .
As soon as she heard about him, a woman whose
little daughter was possessed by an evil spirit
came and fell at his feet.

Mark 7:24–25 NIV

Jesus came to bring the Good News to the Jews
first. But this woman, a Gentile, with a demon-
possessed daughter says she needs Jesus' touch, too.
And He responds to her faith. Ask Jesus to touch
your life this day.

Keeping His Commands

*You shall consecrate yourselves therefore
and be holy, for I am the LORD your God.
You shall keep My statutes and practice them;
I am the LORD who sanctifies you.*

Leviticus 20:7–8

Lord, having a relationship with You is the only
way we can keep Your commands. Help us to
relinquish our wills to You.

Transformation

*Six days later, Jesus took with Him Peter and James
and John. . . . And He was transfigured before them;
and His garments became radiant and exceedingly
white, as no launderer on earth can whiten them.*

Mark 9:2–3

When we come to believe in Him as Lord and
Savior, Christ transforms us, too, quickening our
spirits so that we are destined to spend eternity
with God in heaven. It's a change on the inside
that is displayed on the outside—for the
unbelieving world to see.

Wise Choices

*From the beginning of creation, God made them male
and female. For this reason a man shall leave his father
and mother, and the two shall become one flesh; so they
are no longer two, but one flesh. What therefore God
has joined together, let no man separate.*

Mark 10:6–9

Lord, only You know the physical and mental
abuse some married women have endured.
Heal their pain and show them how to make wise
choices. And forgive me when I miss Your best
for me.

Celebrate!

You shall have the fiftieth year as a jubilee;
you shall not sow, nor reap its aftergrowth,
nor gather in from its untrimmed vines.

Leviticus 25:11

Lord, Your ways are filled with wisdom. If only the world would realize Your majesty! On that day that You create a new heaven and earth, we will know what it really means to celebrate!

A Legacy of Love

The memory of the righteous is blessed,
but the name of the wicked will rot.

Proverbs 10:7

To leave a rich legacy of love one must be dearly
acquainted with the Author of Love, our heavenly
Father. Lord, help me to live in such a worthy
manner that I might be remembered as following
after You all my days.

His Workmanship

*For we are His workmanship, created in Christ Jesus
for good works, which God prepared beforehand
so that we would walk in them.*
Ephesians 2:10

Only when I came to Christ, in a Christian
commitment of faith, did I finally realize the
importance of being a woman. All of the talents
and resources God has built into each of us are
essential—to love a husband, maintain a home,
nurture children so they exhibit godly behavior,
and perform specific tasks here on earth.

Hope of Eternal Life

*And again He took the twelve aside and began to
tell them what was going to happen to Him, saying,
"Behold, we are going up to Jerusalem, and the Son
of Man will be delivered to the chief priests and the
scribes, and they will condemn Him to death. . .and
three days later He will rise again."*
Mark 10:32–34

Lord, when grief overwhelms us let us remember
Your death on Calvary's cross provides our hope of
eternal life in heaven.

A Plan for All Things

*"Take a census of all the congregation of the sons of
Israel, by their families, by their fathers' households,
according to the number of names, every male, head by
head from twenty years old and upward, whoever is able
to go out to war in Israel, you and Aaron shall number
them by their armies."*

Numbers 1:2–3

Lord, with You everything has a plan. In a world
that is filled with nebulous thinking I can rely on
Your consistency.

The Lord Knows Your Heart

*The chief priests and the scribes and the elders
came to Him, and began saying to Him, "By what
authority are You doing these things, or who gave
You this authority to do these things?"*

Mark 11:27–28

Jesus Christ cannot be fooled. He knew the hearts
of the Pharisees and scribes and He knows your
heart, too. Jesus, You spoke plainly about who You
are. Help me hear.

Grant Me Strength

Again the LORD spoke to Moses, saying,
"Speak to the sons of Israel and say to them,
'When a man or woman makes a special vow,
the vow of a Nazirite, to dedicate himself to the LORD,
he shall abstain from wine and strong drink.'"

Numbers 6:1–3

Whatever is preventing me from seeing only You,
Lord, provide the strength I require to set it aside.

Time to Know God

*And Jesus began to say, as He taught in the temple,
"How is it that the scribes say that the Christ is the
son of David? . . . David himself calls Him 'Lord'; so in
what sense is He his son?" And the large crowd
enjoyed listening to Him.*

Mark 12:35–37

Am I like those in the crowd who simply "enjoyed
listening" to Christ? Help me take time to know
You, Lord.

"Fear of the Lord"

The fear of the LORD prolongs life, but the years of the wicked will be shortened. The hope of the righteous is gladness, but the expectation of the wicked perishes.

Proverbs 10:27–28

Instead of being a cause of terror in our hearts, that phrase, "fear of the Lord," means to reverence and honor Him as God. God's very nature is goodness. Therefore, everything that stems from Him reflects His character. This knowledge should cause hope to flood our lives.

More Effective

Behold, I was brought forth in iniquity,
and in sin my mother conceived me.
Psalm 51:5

Admitting our own sinful state is the first step
toward a more sincere Christian walk. And
acknowledging the sin in our children makes us
more effective Christian parents.

Always in Our Best Interest

Then the LORD came down in a pillar of cloud and stood at the doorway of the tent, and He called Aaron and Miriam. When they had both come forward, He said, "Hear now My words: If there is a prophet among you, I, the LORD, shall make Myself known to him in a vision. I shall speak with him in a dream."

Numbers 12:5–6

Lord, although it's human to question things beyond my control, please help me understand that Your actions are always in my best interest.

Believe

*Peter had followed Him at a distance, right into the
courtyard of the high priest; and he was sitting with the
officers and warming himself at the fire. Now the chief
priests and the whole Council kept trying to obtain
testimony against Jesus to put Him to death,
and they were not finding any.*

Mark 14:54–55

Lord, I believe in all that You are, both God and
Man.

Surrender

Now Korah. . .took action. . . .
They assembled together against Moses and Aaron,
and said to them, "You have gone far enough,
for all the congregation are holy, every one
of them, and the LORD is in their midst;
so why do you exalt yourselves above the
assembly of the LORD?"
Numbers 16:1–3

Like Korah, do you fight for control of your life?
Surrender the ultimate control to God and realize
the freedom of His perfect plan.

Today, Lord

*Pilate answered them, saying, "Do you want
me to release for you the King of the Jews?"
But the chief priests stirred up the crowd to
ask him to release Barabbas for them instead.
They shouted back, "Crucify Him!"*
Mark 15.9, 11, 13

What would I have shouted if I had been part of
that crowd? And what affirmation do I give You
today, Lord?

Preparation

Joseph of Arimathea came, a prominent member of the Council, who himself was waiting for the kingdom of God; and he gathered up courage and went in before Pilate, and asked for the body of Jesus.

Mark 15:43

Joseph was "a good and righteous man" (Luke 23:50). He had been born again through his faith in Christ. And knowing the scriptures concerning the death of his Savior, he prepared for it.

The Fulfillment

*"Speak to the sons of Israel that they bring you an
unblemished red heifer in which is no defect and on
which a yoke has never been placed." And it shall be
brought outside the camp and be slaughtered.*

Numbers 19:2–3

The purpose of everything God told the Israelites
to do was to point the way to Christ. Help me,
Lord, to see the Old Testament in light of the
New Testament. For Christ is the fulfillment of
all I seek.

My Refuge and Strength

When I am afraid, I will put my trust in You. In God,
whose word I praise, in God I have put my trust; I shall
not be afraid. What can mere man do to me?
Psalm 56:3–4

Where do you go for refuge? I run to the arms
of my loving Father, just as David did in his own
crisis. And He always comes through. O Lord,
You alone are my refuge and strength.

Restore My Hope

In the days of Herod, king of Judea, there was a certain priest named Zacharias. . .and he had a wife. . .and her name was Elizabeth. They were both righteous in the sight of God, walking blamelessly in all the commandments and requirements of the Lord. But they had no child, because Elizabeth was barren, and they were both advanced in years.

Luke 1:5–7

What the world would have lost if Zacharias had become bitter over his circumstances! Lord, restore my hope in You today.

Beacon of Truth

*So Israel joined themselves to Baal of Peor,
and the LORD was angry against Israel.
And the LORD said to Moses, "Take all the leaders
of the people and execute them in broad daylight
before the LORD, so that the fierce anger of the
LORD may turn away from Israel."*

Numbers 25:3–4

Lord, shine Your beacon of truth on those who
are in leadership, that they may never lead others
astray.

Blessed by God

*And there was a prophetess, Anna. . . . She was
advanced in years. . . . She never left the temple,
serving night and day with fastings and prayers.
At that very moment she came up and began
giving thanks to God.*

Luke 2:36–38

God had promised Anna that she would see the
Messiah before she died. She waited eighty-four
years, and He kept His Word. Let us strive to
follow Anna's prayerful example, and we, too, will
be blessed by God.

Sure of Commitment

Then the LORD spoke to Moses, saying,
"Among these the land shall be divided for an
inheritance according to the number of names."
Numbers 26:52–53

One day Christ Himself will return to claim the
Holy Land for His people. He is coming back
as the ultimate Judge and Rescuer of Israel. The
time is now to be sure of our commitment to Jesus
Christ and that of our loved ones.

The Word. . .and Love

The word of God came to John, the son of Zacharias,
in the wilderness. And he came into all the district
around the Jordan, preaching a baptism of repentance
for the forgiveness of sins.
Luke 3:2–3

John's exhortations were aimed at the "wilderness
of men's souls." Many claim the faith yet exist in a
wasteland of sin. Lord, help me to proclaim Your
World and love to anyone, anywhere.

Lead Me to the Rock

Hear my cry, O God; give heed to my prayer.
From the end of the earth I call to You when my heart
is faint; lead me to the rock that is higher than I.
For You have been a refuge for me, a tower of strength
against the enemy. . . . Let me take refuge in the
shelter of Your wings.

Psalm 61:1–4

Lord, I search for a way through the torrents of
despair. How precious is the knowledge that You
hear and care.

Obedience

[The sons of Israel]. . .journeyed from Rameses in the first month, on the fifteenth day of the first month; on the next day after the Passover the sons of Israel started out boldly in the sight of all the Egyptians, while the Egyptians were burying all their firstborn.

Numbers 33:3–4

At times, Israel's hardships made them long to be back in the bondage in Egypt. But much of their pain was because they refused to obey.

Equally Yoked

*Every daughter who comes into possession of an
inheritance of any tribe of the sons of Israel shall be
wife to one of the family of the tribe of her father, so
that the sons of Israel each may possess the inheritance
of his fathers. Thus no inheritance shall be transferred
from one tribe to another tribe.*

Numbers 36:8–9

Lord, we know that Joseph loved Mary and both
were chosen by You. Yet they also obeyed You in
their choice of a life partner.

Perfect Victory

And the devil said to Him, "If You are the
Son of God, tell this stone to become bread."
And Jesus answered him, "It is written,
'Man shall not live on bread alone.' "

Luke 4:3–4

Have you ever found yourself so tempted to sin
that you ached all the way to your soul? Christ
understands that pull toward evil. Lord, I thank
You for Your Son's perfect victory over Satan.

Time to Praise

*Shout joyfully to God, all the earth; sing the glory
of His name; make His praise glorious.*

Psalm 66:1–2

David knew even in his day that taking time to
praise His awesome God provided strength and
renewal for his weary soul. Lord, my grateful
heart declares Your Name in a world that has all
but forgotten You still care and watch over the
universe.

"Follow Me"

After that He went out, and noticed a
tax collector named Levi sitting in the tax booth,
and He said to him, "Follow Me." . . . And Levi
gave a big reception for Him in his house; and there
was a great crowd of tax collectors and other people
who were reclining at the table with them.
Luke 5:27–29

Christ's presence at this reception provided an
opportunity for Him to share the gospel message.
We, too, can seek out those whom society shuns
and offer the compassion of Christ.

Unwavering Trust

*The LORD your God has multiplied you, and behold,
you are this day like the stars of heaven in number.
May the LORD, the God of your fathers, increase you a
thousand-fold more than you are and bless you
just as He has promised you!*

Deuteronomy 1:10–11

Dear heavenly Father, let my trust in You never
waver. Give me wisdom and courage for this day.

Solitude

It was at this time that He went off to the mountain to pray, and He spent the whole night in prayer to God. And when day came, He called His disciples to Him and chose twelve of them, whom He also named as apostles.

Luke 6:12–13

Christ prayed all night for the men who would preach, teach, heal the sick, raise the dead, and record His words. When it's time to do battle, we need to be alone first.

"A Father to the Fatherless"

A father of the fatherless and a judge for the widows,
is God in His holy habitation.
Psalm 68:5

God has promised to be "a father to the fatherless."
If you're a single mom, count on Him to keep His
Word. And instead of attempting to be both father
and mother, you can just be a mom to your kids.
Lord, help me to entrust all my heavy burdens to
Your care.

Always and Forever

Hear, O Israel! The LORD is our God,
the LORD is one!

Deuteronomy 6:4

Throughout the scriptures there are references
to the contributions of the Triune God. While
the Father spoke from heaven, confirming
Christ at His baptism, the Holy Spirit descended
upon Christ as a dove. Only God could have
omnisciently conceived of the Trinity. God has
always been, and will forever be.

Proclaim the Kingdom

And He called the twelve together, and gave them power and authority over all the demons and to heal diseases. And He sent them out to proclaim the kingdom of God and to perform healing.

Luke 9:1–2

Lord, how grateful I am that Your Holy Spirit worked in the lives of these apostles, molding them into strong men of faith. Help me to become unselfish with my time that many more will hear the gospel.

Give God the Glory

*When you enter the land which the LORD
your God gives you, you shall not learn to imitate
the detestable things of those nations. For whoever
does these things is detestable to the LORD;
and because of these detestable things the LORD
your God will drive them out before you.*

Deuteronomy 18:9, 12

Is God receiving all the glory in your life? Lord,
You know better than I what things will draw my
time and attention away from You. Give me the
courage to obey You.

Confirmed Reservation

And behold, two men were talking with Him;
and they were Moses and Elijah, who, appearing
in glory, were speaking of His departure which
He was about to accomplish at Jerusalem.

Luke 9:30–31

In case you've been feeling sorry for Moses, who
never got to enter the Promised Land, just look
at what God had in store for him. O Lord, I am
so grateful that our place with You is already
reserved!

The Rock

*Be to me a rock of habitation to which I may
continually come; You have given commandment to
save me, for You are my rock and my fortress.*

Psalm 71:3

Over fifty times in scripture the word *rock* is used
in reference to God. When everything else fails,
He is steadfast, immovable, and unchangeable.

A Better Witness

But it shall come about, if you do not obey the LORD your God, to observe to do all His commandments and His statutes with which I charge you today, that all these curses will come upon you and overtake you.

Deuteronomy 28:15

Lord, the people of Noah's day refused to heed his preaching. Help me to be a better witness before time again runs out.

Take Time

A woman named Martha welcomed Him into her home. She had a sister called Mary, who was seated at the Lord's feet, listening to His word. But Martha was distracted with all her preparations; and she came up to Him and said, "Lord, do You not care that my sister has left me to do all the serving alone?"

Luke 10:38–40

Have you taken time to get to know your Lord? Perhaps your life, like Martha's, is missing the best part.

With All Your Heart

Moreover the LORD your God will circumcise your heart and the heart of your descendants, to love the LORD your God with all your heart and with all your soul, so that you may live.

Deuteronomy 30:6

Father, I know circumcision of my heart is wrought by Your Holy Spirit. Lord, make me willing to undergo transformation that I might truly love You, and others.

Content of the Heart

Listen, O my people, to my instruction; incline your ears to the words of my mouth. I will open my mouth in a parable; I will utter dark sayings of old, which we have heard and known, and our fathers have told us.

Psalm 78:1–3

When you examine the content of my heart, Lord, which type of soil have I prepared for Your Word?

Chosen by God

Then Moses called to Joshua and said to him in the sight of all Israel, "Be strong and courageous, for you shall go with this people into the land which the LORD has sworn to their fathers to give them, and you shall give it to them as an inheritance."

Deuteronomy 31:7

Lord, I forget sometimes that those in leadership are chosen by You. And with responsibility comes accountability.

Everyone

And I say to you, everyone who confesses Me before men, the Son of Man will confess him also before the angels of God; but he who denies Me before men will be denied before the angels of God.

Luke 12:8- 9

All men are in need of a Savior. And the Bible states clearly that only one person fills this job description. "And there is salvation in no one else" (Acts 4:12). Jesus Christ is that Savior.

Wet Cement

He who withholds his rod hates his son,
but he who loves him disciplines him diligently.

Proverbs 13:24

"Discipline" is meant to teach the correct behavior. "Punishment" only makes a child bitter. Lord, help me to remember what Anne Ortlund teaches, that children are wet cement. Assist me in making good impressions on their lives.

Let God Steer the Course

*O Jerusalem, Jerusalem, you who kill the prophets
and stone those sent to you, how often I have longed
to gather your children together, as a hen gathers her
chicks under her wings, but you were not willing!*

Luke 13:34 NIV

How like the Israelites I am! God showed them the
path they were to walk in. And yet time after time
they leaped beyond the lines of safety and tried
to live without Him. Is it time for you to let God
steer the course?

New Heights

*Now Joshua the son of Nun was filled with the
spirit of wisdom, for Moses had laid his hands on him;
and the sons of Israel listened to him and did as the
LORD had commanded Moses.*

Deuteronomy 34:9

Father, as You did with Joshua, lead me to new
heights in my walk with You.

Deliver Us

*Help us, O God of our salvation, for the glory
of Your name; and deliver us and forgive
our sins for Your name's sake.*

Psalm 79:9

We thank You that we can come to You as Lord
and Messiah. You are truly a God of forgiveness.

True Faith

With cunning they conspire against your people;
they plot against those you cherish. "Come," they say,
"let us destroy them as a nation, that the name of
Israel be remembered no more."
Psalm 83:3–4 NIV

Even in King David's time the survival of the
Jews appeared precarious at best. God spared and
preserved David from invading armies, despite
all odds, and used him to raise up a nation. Lord,
today Your power still sustains the Jews. Give them
true faith!

Use Me, Lord

Then Joshua the son of Nun sent two men
as spies secretly from Shittim, saying,
"Go, view the land, especially Jericho."
So they went and came into the house of a harlot
whose name was Rahab, and lodged there.

Joshua 2:1

Lord, Rahab believed You and You used her to hide
Joshua's spies. How can You use me?

Direct Wisely

Every person is to be in subjection to the governing
authorities. For there is no authority except from
God, and those which exist are established by God.
For because of this you also pay taxes, for rulers are
servants of God, devoting themselves to this very thing.

Romans 13:1, 6

Lord, let me give to the government not
grudgingly but out of obedience to You. And
please assist those in authority over me to direct
wisely the use of these funds.

"Sonbeams"

Or what woman, if she has ten silver coins and loses one coin, does not light a lamp and sweep the house and search carefully until she finds it? When she has found it, she calls together her friends and neighbors, saying, "Rejoice with me."

Luke 15:8–9

Jesus compared the woman's joy to the celebration that goes on in heaven when a sinner repents and "Sonbeams" of peace finally flood the soul. It's the feeling of "wholeness" a person hungers for all her life.

Eternal Destination

*And a poor man named Lazarus was laid at his gate,
covered with sores. Now the poor man died and was
carried away by the angels to Abraham's bosom.*

Luke 16:20, 22

Once life has ceased we no longer have the power
to change our eternal destination. And although
he suffered in life, the poor man now resided in
paradise.

Pave My Way

*Take up for yourselves twelve stones from here
out of the middle of the Jordan, from the place
where the priests' feet are standing firm, and carry
them over with you and lay them down in the lodging
place where you will lodge tonight.*

Joshua 4:3

Lord, please pave my way with stones from
You, stones of dedication, perseverance, and
compassion.

Let the Children Come

And they were bringing children to Him so that He might touch them; and the disciples rebuked them. But when Jesus saw this, He was indignant and said to them, "Permit the children to come to Me; do not hinder them; for the kingdom of God belongs to such as these. Truly I say to you, whoever does not receive the kingdom of God like a child will not enter it at all."

Mark 10:13–15

Lord, only You can offer true comfort to those who have lost little ones.

Winning Strategy

The LORD said to Joshua, "See, I have given Jericho into your hand, with its king and the valiant warriors. You shall march around the city, all the men of war circling the city once. You shall do so for six days."

Joshua 6:2–3

Lord, I need to remember that You're the Lord who not only guarantees victory in the battle, but draws up the winning strategy. Thank You for that assurance.

Real Love

Be on your guard! If your brother sins,
rebuke him; and if he repents, forgive him.

Luke 17:3

Here Jesus admonished His disciples to "rebuke"
their brothers if they've sinned. Why? Because
sin is a progressive fall. And "real love" means
intervening that they might get back on track.

Anticipate the Day

*How lovely are Your dwelling places, O LORD of hosts!
My soul longed and even yearned for the courts
of the LORD; my heart and my flesh sing for joy
to the living God.*

Psalm 84:1–2

How King David must have longed for a lasting
peace. But he had to settle for that little niche of
peace he carved out for himself while pondering
what heaven was like, anticipating the day he'd
dwell with God.

Always with Us

*Then He took the twelve aside and said to them,
"Behold, we are going up to Jerusalem, and all things
which are written through the prophets about the Son
of Man will be accomplished. For He will be handed
over to the Gentiles, and will be mocked and mistreated
and spit upon, and after they have scourged Him, they
will kill Him; and the third day He will rise again."*
Luke 18:31–33

Father, help me realize, like the disciples, that You
are always with me, to the end.

Every Crisis

*Then Joshua spoke to the LORD. . .
in the sight of Israel, "O sun, stand still at Gibeon,
and O moon in the valley of Aijalon." So the sun
stood still, and the moon stopped, until the nation
avenged themselves of their enemies.*
Joshua 10:12–13

If God is able to stop the solar system, He is able
to deal with every crisis in your life.

Justice

In a certain city there was a judge who did not fear
God and did not respect man. There was a widow in
that city, and she kept coming to him, saying, "Give me
legal protection from my opponent."

Luke 18:2–3

Lord, You alone judge rightly. You alone will
administer to the guilty the punishment they truly
deserve.

Soothe and Heal

A wise son accepts his father's discipline, but a scoffer does not listen to rebuke. From the fruit of a man's mouth he enjoys good, but the desire of the treacherous is violence. The one who guards his mouth preserves his life; the one who opens wide his lips comes to ruin.

Proverbs 13:1–3

Each day presents an opportunity to extend to others words that reach in to soothe and heal souls—or deepen wounds.

"Thou Alone"

There is no one like You among the gods, O Lord;
nor are there any works like Yours. For You are great
and do wondrous deeds; You alone are God.
Psalm 86:8,10

Lord, You've given me an entire Bible to read
so that I might learn of Your love, concern,
and compassion. Develop in me that sensitivity
to "hear the prompting of Your Spirit" while You
guide me toward the truth.

Chosen People

*Now these are the territories which the sons
of Israel inherited in the land of Canaan, which
Eleazar the priest, and Joshua the son of Nun,
and the heads of the households of the tribes of
the sons of Israel apportioned to them for an
inheritance, by the lot of their inheritance,
as the LORD commanded through Moses.*

Joshua 14:1–2

Lord, I know that all things work to bring about
Your plan. Please continue to protect Your chosen
people.

God Incarnate

Go into the village ahead of you; there,
as you enter, you will find a colt tied on which
no one yet has ever sat; untie it and bring it here.
If anyone asks you, "Why are you untying it?"
you shall say, "The LORD has need of it."
Luke 19:30–31

Lord, thank You for all the "absolutes" of scripture. I believe You are exactly who You claim to be, God Incarnate.

Staying in God's Will

*Now it came about after the death of Joshua
that the sons of Israel inquired of the LORD,
saying, "Who shall go up first for us against
the Canaanites, to fight against them?"*

Judges 1:1–2

Israel thought they could peacefully coexist with
idol worshipers, but little by little they allowed this
sea of sin to seep under the undergirding of their
own society. When we move away from God's will,
all manner of sin can somehow be justified.

In the Beginning

In the beginning was the Word,
and the Word was with God,
and the Word was God.
He was in the beginning with God.

John 1:1–2

The apostle John was an eyewitness to the events he was inspired by God's Spirit to record for us. "By this you know the Spirit of God: every spirit that confesses that Jesus Christ has come in the flesh is from God" (1 John 4:2).

Rejoice in Worship

*It is good to give thanks to the LORD
and to sing praises to Your name, O Most High;
to declare Your lovingkindness in the morning
and Your faithfulness by night.*

Psalm 92:1–2

Lord, thank You for music and the way it uplifts
my spirits. No matter what time of day or season,
I rejoice in worshiping You.

"Building Codes"

The wise woman builds her house,
but the foolish tears it down with her own hands.

Proverbs 14:1

Every woman must understand God's "building codes" in order to strengthen her own household. Lord, You are the master builder. To stay upright I must follow Your blueprints.

A Fresh Start

*And the Word became flesh, and dwelt among us,
and we beheld His glory, glory as of the only begotten
from the Father, full of grace and truth.*

John 1:14

It's our nature to sin. And that's why we need a
new nature. This is exactly what Christ purchased
for us on Calvary's cross, the right to be indwelt
with the very Spirit of God. A fresh start, isn't that
what all of us are seeking?

Strength for Obedience

*I brought you up out of Egypt and led you into
the land which I have sworn to your fathers;
and I said, "I will never break My covenant with you,
and as for you, you shall make no covenant with the
inhabitants of this land; you shall tear down their
altars." But you have not obeyed Me.*

Judges 2:1–2

Lord, cleanse my soul and fill me with Your
strength that I might not backslide into the pit of
disobedience again.

A Wisdom-Filled Heart

*Wisdom reposes in the heart of the discerning
and even among fools she lets herself be known.*
Proverbs 14:33 NIV

Although we can't change others' hearts, our own
can be filled with wisdom. Confident in our eternal
destination, we can exude serenity, peace, and love.

Hunger for Daily Worship

Now the sons of Israel again did evil in the sight of the LORD. So the LORD strengthened Eglon the king of Moab against Israel, because they had done evil in the sight of the LORD. . . . The sons of Israel served Eglon the king of Moab eighteen years.

Judges 3:12–14

Lord, please instill in me a hunger for daily study and worship, that I might not sin.

Living Bread

They asked, and He brought quail,
and satisfied them with the bread of heaven.
Psalm 105:40

Lord, I long for the living bread. I long to live
forever in Your glorious presence.

Help Me to Listen. . .

They asked him, "What then? Are you Elijah?"
And he said, "I am not."
John 1:21

Father, Jesus and John the Baptist delivered
the truth of Your Word, but people refused to
heed their messages. Lord, help me to listen and
respond.

Commit Your Works

The plans of the heart belong to man,
but the answer of the tongue is from the LORD.
All the ways of a man are clean in his own sight,
but the LORD weighs the motives.
Commit your works to the LORD
and your plans will he established.

Proverbs 16:1–3

Lord, there have been times when I compromised the Truth of Your Word. Please help me get back on track. Place my feet firmly on the pavement of Your Word.

Wise Women

Now Deborah, a prophetess, the wife of Lappidoth, was judging Israel at that time. She used to sit under the palm tree of Deborah between Ramah and Bethel in the hill country of Ephraim; and the sons of Israel came up to her for judgment.

Judges 4:4–5

Lord, thank You for using a woman to save Israel!

This Is the Day

*Arise! For this is the day in which
the LORD has given Sisera into your hands;
behold, the LORD has gone out before you.*

Judges 4:14

God began to display His awesome power. A great
storm arose, and the rain and hail pelted the faces of
Sisera's troops, rendering vision impossible. Israel,
with their backs to the storm, began to attack.
Meanwhile, Sisera fled on foot and was killed by a
woman. Deborah's prophecy had come true.

Day 134

Beautiful and Holy

*The LORD says to my Lord: "Sit at My right hand until
I make Your enemies a footstool for Your feet."*
Psalm 110:1

Father, I thank You that I can call You many
names, and all of them are beautiful and holy.

Share the Love

He found first his own brother Simon
and said to him, "We have found the Messiah"
(which translated means Christ).

John 1:41

How blessed for Andrew that his brother
responded and they shared the love of the Lord
together. Lord, I pray for strength to share Your
love with unbelieving family members.

The Cornerstone

*The stone which the builders rejected
has become the chief corner stone.*

Psalm 118:22

When a building is started, a cornerstone must be placed precisely, because the rest of the structure is lined up with it. Lord Jesus Christ, You alone are to be the cornerstone of my life. Please help me to discard those concerns that block my view of You.

Sharing the Word

The LORD will tear down the house of the proud,
but He will establish the boundary of the widow.

Proverbs 15:25

Father, let me share Your Word with those women
who now find themselves alone—"Now she who is
a widow indeed and who has been left alone, has
fixed her hope on God and continues in entreaties
and prayers night and day" (1 Timothy 5:5).

Message of Assurance

Gideon was beating out wheat in the wine press in order to save it from the Midianites. The angel of the LORD appeared to him and said to him, "The LORD is with you, O valiant warrior."

Judges 6:11–12

Have you ever felt that the weight of the world rested on your shoulders? Well, that's Gideon for you. The Lord gave Gideon the same resounding message of assurance that He always gives to His servants: that He was with Him and that was enough.

A God of Miracles

*When the wine ran out, the mother of Jesus
said to Him, "They have no wine."*
John 2:3

Father, You are still the God of miracles. I thank
You that You know my needs.

Day 140

Teach Me Your Ways, Lord

*I have told of my ways, and You have answered me;
teach me Your statutes. Make me understand the way
of Your precepts, so I will meditate on Your wonders.*
Psalm 119:26–27

Lord, teach me Your ways, that I might live out
Your precepts before my family and loved ones.

Trustworthy

When a wicked man comes, contempt also comes,
and with dishonor comes scorn.
Proverbs 18:3

Women become vulnerable the instant truth is replaced with desire. It's like when the tip of an arrow finds the one small point of vulnerability and penetrates a suit of armor. Lord, sometimes I want so badly to be loved that I trust the wrong people. Please guide me to those who are trustworthy.

Second Chances

*Jesus answered and said to him, "Truly, truly,
I say to you, unless one is born again
he cannot see the kingdom of God."*

John 3:3

Lord, You told Nicodemus he must be born again.
I praise You that You are the God of second
chances, the God of truth!

On Our Side

*The LORD said to Gideon, "The people who are
with you are too many for Me to give Midian into
their hands, lest Israel become boastful, saying,
'My own power has delivered me.' Now therefore come,
proclaim in the hearing of the people, saying,
'Whoever is afraid and trembling, let him return
and depart from Mount Gilead.'" So 22,000
people returned, but 10,000 remained.*

Judges 7:2–3

If God is on our side, we don't need anyone else.

Day 144

A Definite Purpose

Your eyes have seen my unformed substance; and in
Your book were all written the days that were ordained
for me, when as yet there was not one of them.

Psalm 139:16

God has a definite purpose for your life. He wants
to use your life to further His kingdom. And if you
are in His will, the last page will have a very happy
ending!

A Virtuous Wife

An excellent wife, who can find? For her worth is far above jewels. The heart of her husband trusts in her, and he will have no lack of gain. She does him good and not evil all the days of her life.

Proverbs 31:10–12

Lord, forgive my selfish tendencies and show me the path to virtue.

Assurance of Eternal Life

He who believes in the Son has eternal life;
but he who does not obey the Son shall not see life,
but the wrath of God abides on him.

John 3:36

The Word of God says that we can have absolute assurance of eternal life today. As we grasp that truth, our lives are transformed.

A God of Justice

*Speak, now, in the hearing of all the leaders
of Shechem, "Which is better for you, that seventy
men, all the sons of Jerubbaal, rule over you, or that
one man rule over you?" Also, remember that
I am your bone and your flesh.*

Judges 9:2

The God of justice always intervenes to bring the
course of history in line with His own design.
Lord, Your eyes see everything. You are a God of
unswerving justice.

Praise Him

*Praise the LORD! Praise God in His sanctuary;
praise Him in His mighty expanse. Praise Him for
His mighty deeds; praise Him according to His
excellent greatness. Let everything that has breath
praise the LORD. Praise the LORD!*

Psalm 150:1–2, 6

In other words, "Praise Him with all you've got to
make noise with!" Isn't that what true worship is,
using our entire beings to give Him the glory He
deserves?

"Give Me a Drink"

*So He came to a city of Samaria called Sychar, near
the parcel of ground that Jacob gave to his son Joseph;
and Jacob's well was there. So Jesus, being wearied from
His journey, was sitting thus by the well. It was about
the sixth hour. There came a woman of Samaria to
draw water. Jesus said to her, "Give Me a drink."*

John 4:5–7

Lord, help me to seek out those who for whatever
reason are shunned and despised. They need You
so much.

Look to God

Then it shall be that whatever comes out of the doors of my house to meet me when I return in peace from the sons of Ammon, it shall be the LORD's, and I will offer it up as a burnt offering. . . . When Jephthah came to his house at Mizpah, behold, his daughter was coming out to meet him with tambourines and with dancing.

Judges 11:31–34

Lord, help me turn to You for my deliverance and not make hasty, costly vows.

From God's Perspective

The words of the Preacher, the son of David,
king in Jerusalem. "Vanity of vanities," says the
Preacher, "Vanity of vanities! All is vanity."

Ecclesiastes 1:1–2

Solomon had experienced the best the world had
to offer. . .and it wasn't enough. Lord, please help
me view my priorities from Your perspective.

Living Water

*Now there is in Jerusalem by the sheep gate a pool. . .
having five porticoes. In these lay a multitude of those
who were sick, blind, lame, and withered, [waiting for
the moving of the waters. . .whoever then first, after the
stirring up of the water, stepped in was made well.]*
John 5:2–4

Lord, if sin is at the root of my infirmity, then
bring me to swift repentance. But if my suffering is
to point others toward Your glory, quench my thirst
with Your living water.

Daily Prayer

*Now Ibzan of Bethlehem judged Israel after him.
He had thirty sons, and thirty daughters whom he
gave in marriage outside the family, and he brought
in thirty daughters from outside for his sons.*

Judges 12:8–9

What other tangible effects of his presence on
earth did this judge of Israel leave behind? How
can we discern the will of God for our lives? Daily
prayer is definitely the main source, not only
relating our needs to God, but also listening for
His directions.

Desire God's Presence

I said to myself, "Come now, I will test you with pleasure. So enjoy yourself." And behold, it too was futility. I said of laughter, "It is madness," and of pleasure, "What does it accomplish?"

Ecclesiastes 2:1–2

Lord, help me not to be drawn away from You by the endless pursuit of things. Instead, I desire Your presence, guidance, and wisdom.

Fully God, Fully Man

*As the living Father sent Me, and I live because
of the Father, so he who eats Me, he also will live
because of Me. This is the bread which came down
out of heaven; not as the fathers ate and died;
he who eats this bread will live forever."*

John 6:57–58

To truly partake of Christ is to accept Him as He
is, fully God and fully man. He was sent from
God, who recognized our need for Him.

Open My Eyes, Lord

*Then the angel of the LORD appeared to the woman,
and said to her, "Behold now, you are barren
and have borne no children, but you shall conceive
and give birth to a son."*

Judges 13:3

Once again, God was about to raise up a deliverer
for Israel. Lord, as I read Your Word, open my eyes
to Your infinite wisdom and understanding.

God's Greatest Gift

*When the sons of Ammon fought against Israel,
the elders of Gilead went to get Jephthah
from the land of Tob.*

Judges 11:5

As women, it's up to us to uphold the sanctity
of life. Each life comes into this world with a
purpose. Therefore, when that life is abruptly
ended, so are all the accomplishments that were
intended for this unique person. Lord, give me
words to describe Your greatest gift—life.

God's Timing

Now the feast of the Jews, the Feast of Booths, was near. Therefore His brothers said to Him, "Leave here and go into Judea, so that Your disciples also may see Your works which You are doing. . . ." For not even His brothers were believing in Him.

John 7:2–5

Thank You, Jesus, for reminding me to wait for God's timing in my life, especially when the pressure applied by others would have me rush on ahead.

Discernment

*Then the woman gave birth to a son and named
him Samson; and the child grew up
and the LORD blessed him.*

Judges 13:24

As Samson struck out on his own, the first thing
he did was fall in love with a Philistine woman.
Although his parents cautioned him against
marrying a pagan, he was determined. Samson's
misuse of power caused the Philistines to kill his
bride and her father. Lord, I pray for discernment
in my own life that I may prosper and not selfishly
hurt others.

A Time for Everything

There is an appointed time for everything. And there is a
time for every event under heaven. A time to weep and a
time to laugh; a time to mourn and a time to dance.

Ecclesiastes 3:1, 4

Once we've finally accepted that God truly loves
us, it's hard to face the first discouraging episode
of tragedy that follows. Lord, through my veil of
tears help me to view Your rescuing hand, that I
might reach out to grasp You more firmly.

Forgiveness—No Matter What

The scribes and the Pharisees brought a woman caught
in adultery, and having set her in the center of the
court, they said to Him, "Teacher, this woman has been
caught in adultery, in the very act. Now in the Law
Moses commanded us to stone such women;
what then do You say?"

John 8:3–5

Lord, forgive me, no matter what my sin, that I
might turn from it and faithfully serve You.

Consistent

Now Samson lay until midnight, and at midnight he arose and took hold of the doors of the city gate and the two posts and pulled them up along with the bars. . . . After this it came about that he loved a woman in the valley of Sorek, whose name was Delilah.

Judges 16:3–4

Lord, give me the gift of discernment that my life may be a consistent testimony of my love for You.

Turn It Around

*Remember also your Creator in the days of your youth,
before the evil days come and the years draw near
when you will say, "I have no delight in them."
Fear God and keep His commandments,
because this applies to every person.*

Ecclesiastes 12:1, 13

Have you forgotten the God of your youth?
Have His principles been compromised away
by the pressures of a world that teaches the Ten
Commandments are optional? With the Lord's
help, it's not too late to turn it all around.

Shake It Up!

As He passed by, He saw a man blind from birth.
And His disciples asked Him, "Rabbi, who sinned,
this man or his parents, that he would be born blind?"
Jesus answered, "It was neither. . .but it was so that the
works of God might be displayed in him."
John 9:1–3

Rather than believe that this man had been healed,
the Pharisees donned their mask of spiritual
blindness. No miracle of God was about to
shake up their world! Lord, open my eyes to Your
miracles.

A Glorious Plan

*Then Elimelech, Naomi's husband, died; and she
was left with her two sons. They took for themselves
Moabite women as wives; the name of the one was
Orpah and the name of the other Ruth.*

Ruth 1:3–4

Few daughters-in-law would have persisted in
devotion to a woman whose life held such abysmal
tragedy and so little prospect for change. However,
God had a glorious plan. Ruth would become
Boaz's bride and mother to his son, whose lineage
would include the Messiah, Jesus Christ.

Persistent Prayers

She, greatly distressed, prayed to the LORD and wept bitterly. She made a vow and said, "O LORD of hosts, if You will indeed look on the affliction of Your maidservant and remember me, and not forget Your maidservant, but will give Your maidservant a son, then I will give him to the LORD all the days of his life."
1 Samuel 1:10–11

The persistent prayers of a Christian woman should never be underestimated!

Faithfully Devoted

My beloved responded and said to me, "Arise, my darling, my beautiful one, and come along. For behold, the winter is past, the rain is over and gone. The flowers have already appeared in the land; the time has arrived for pruning the vines, and the voice of the turtledove has been heard in our land. . . . Arise, my darling, my beautiful one, and come along!"
Song of Solomon 2:10–13

Lord, make me a woman who is faithfully devoted to You.

By Name

*But he who enters by the door is a shepherd
of the sheep. To him the doorkeeper opens,
and the sheep hear his voice, and he calls his
own sheep by name, and leads them out.*

John 10:2–3

God calls us by name, just as the shepherd has
pet names for his sheep. Someday, when the King
of kings, our Good Shepherd, calls us home to
heaven, we'll hear the name He calls us.

Sincere Faithfulness

It came about in due time, after Hannah had conceived,
that she gave birth to a son; and she named him
Samuel, saying, "Because I have asked him
of the LORD."
1 Samuel 1:20

Lord, if You should give me a child, guide me as
You guided Hannah—to sincere faithfulness.

Open My Mind, Lord

*The vision of Isaiah the son of Amoz concerning
Judah and Jerusalem. . . . Listen, O heavens, and hear,
O earth; for the LORD speaks, "Sons I have reared
and brought up, but they have revolted against Me. . . .
My people do not understand."*

Isaiah 1:1–3

Lord, this book of prophecy displays Your
promises and prophecies. Open my mind to
receive Your truth. And keep me from confusion,
that I might know You as both Messiah and Lord.

Strengthen My Faith

Now a certain man was sick, Lazarus of Bethany. . . .
The sisters sent word to Him, saying, "LORD, behold,
he whom You love is sick."
John 11:1, 3

Have you allowed Christ to exercise His authority
to bring you forth to new life? Lord, strengthen
my faith so that when tragedy strikes, I know that
You are the Resurrection and the Life.

Our Rock

Then Hannah prayed and said, "My heart exults in the
LORD; my horn is exalted in the LORD. . . . There is no
one holy like the LORD, indeed, there is no one besides
You, nor is there any rock like our God."
1 Samuel 2:1–2

Hannah spent her time in the temple, praying
and serving others. And God granted the deepest
longing of her heart, despite the fact that she was
just a sinner who could offer God nothing but her
brokenness and yielded spirit.

Light of Truth

Unless the LORD of hosts had left us a few survivors,
we would be like Sodom, we would be like Gomorrah.
Hear the word of the LORD, you rulers of Sodom;
give ear to the instruction of our God,
you people of Gomorrah.

Isaiah 1:9–10

Lord, thank You for sending Your messengers to
minister to my heart. Through them the light of
Your truth finally dawned in my heart. Thank You
for Your peace.

Never for Granted

Mary then took a pound of very costly perfume of pure nard, and anointed the feet of Jesus and wiped His feet with her hair; and the house was filled with the fragrance of the perfume.

John 12:3

Lord, let me never take You for granted.

Instill Obedience

Thus says the LORD, "Did I not indeed reveal Myself
to the house of your father when they were in Egypt in
bondage to Pharaoh's house? Did I not choose them
from all the tribes of Israel to be My priests. . . ?
Why do you kick at My sacrifice and at
My offering which I have commanded in My dwelling,
and honor your sons above Me?"

1 Samuel 2:27–29

Lord, instill obedience in me also.

Take Charge

For You have abandoned Your people, the house of Jacob,
because they are filled with influences from the east,
and they are soothsayers like the Philistines, and they
strike bargains with the children of foreigners. . . .
Their land has also been filled with idols; they worship the
work of their hands, that which their fingers have made.

Isaiah 2:6–8

Lord, be in charge of my own priority list.

The Light of the World

He who believes in Me, does not believe in Me but in Him who sent Me. He who sees Me sees the One who sent Me. I have come as Light into the world, so that everyone who believes in Me will not remain in darkness.
John 12:44–46

Your truth is readily available, Lord. Therefore, I know with certainty that I will one day see You face-to-face. Deepen my faith so that I might penetrate the spiritual darkness around me.

"Here I Am"

The LORD called Samuel; and he said, "Here I am."
1 Samuel 3:4

Lord, keep me close to You, that I may always hear You.

God's Word Fulfilled

*Therefore the LORD Himself will give you a sign:
Behold, a virgin will be with child and bear a son,
and she will call His name Immanuel.*

Isaiah 7:14

This prediction of Christ's conception was delivered over seven hundred years before He was actually born. In announcing to Joseph that Mary was with child by the power of God's Spirit, the angel used these exact words from Isaiah. Lord, thank You that what You have said always comes to pass.

Called to Be Servants

Jesus, knowing that the Father had given all things into His hands, and that He had come forth from God, and was going back to God, got up from supper, and laid aside His garments; and taking a towel, He girded Himself.

John 13:3–4

How difficult it must have been for Christ to say good-bye to His disciples, knowing they still didn't fully comprehend His impending death! So Jesus set about to love them and to show them that they were likewise called to be servants.

The Promise

The oracle concerning Babylon which Isaiah the son of Amoz saw. Lift up a standard on the bare hill, raise your voice to them. . . . Wail, for the day of the LORD is near! It will come as destruction from the Almighty.

Isaiah 13:1–2, 6

There is a specific time in history when the final judgment against the disobedient will take place. Lord, thank You for Your Word that contains not only the promise of salvation, but the promise of judgment.

Our Mansion

In My Father's house are many dwelling places;
if it were not so, I would have told you;
for I go to prepare a place for you.

John 14:2

Jesus Christ has promised to prepare a place for us in heaven. The only problem is that we have to wait down here until He's got our mansion ready for us. Lord, thank You for the Holy Spirit, who brings us peace and comfort until we can be united with You in heaven.

The Lord's Presence

So the Philistines fought and Israel was defeated,
and every man fled to his tent; and the slaughter
was very great. . . . And the ark of God was taken.
1 Samuel 4:10–11

As long as the Israelites kept the ark of God with
them, they were invincible to the nations that
sought to conquer them, for the Lord's presence
was among them. Because they had forsaken God,
He was about to teach them what life would be like
without Him on their side.

Lord, Give Me Insight

And it came about when Samuel was old that he
appointed his sons judges over Israel. . . . His sons,
however, did not walk in his ways.

1 Samuel 8:1, 3

Seeing the wickedness of Samuel's sons, the elders
of Israel asked for a human king, so they might
be "like all the nations." But they'd always been
the envy of these other nations, which knew that
Israel's king was God Almighty. Lord, give me
insight to make You king of my life.

Abide in the Vine

"As the branch cannot bear fruit of itself unless it abides
in the vine, so neither can you unless you abide in Me.
I am the vine, you are the branches; he who abides in
Me, and I in him, he bears much fruit, for apart from
Me you can do nothing."

John 15:4–5

The same offer to abide in the vine is extended
to all who hear the gospel message. Have you
responded? How diligently are you abiding?

My Redeemer

Then the glory of the LORD will be revealed,
and all flesh will see it together;
for the mouth of the LORD has spoken.

Isaiah 40:5

Only when we are totally dependent on our Redeemer are we truly free! Lord Jesus, I rejoice that You came to be my Redeemer. Hallelujah! Amen!

Changed By Love

*The nations will see your righteousness,
and all kings your glory; and you will be called by a new
name which the mouth of the LORD will designate.*

Isaiah 62:2

Whenever God sets about to perform a work of
regeneration He also provides a new name. Lord,
my name remains the same, but my heart is forever
changed by Your love.

The Holy Spirit

It is to your advantage that I go away;
for if I do not go away, the Helper will not come to you;
but if I go, I will send Him to you.

John 16:7

The Holy Spirit was presented to the disciples as a tongue of fire, that they might have proof of His appearance. He would be with them every moment to guide, and to convict the world concerning sin, righteousness, and judgment. Are you aware of these things in your own life?

Fully Committed

He had a son whose name was Saul, a choice and handsome man, and there was not a more handsome person than he among the sons of Israel; from his shoulders and up he was taller than any of the people.

1 Samuel 9:2

Outward appearance means nothing if that person isn't fully committed to God. God chose Saul to be Israel's king so that this nation might eventually learn their need for spiritual discernment.

True Worship

Thus says the LORD, "Heaven is My throne, and the earth is My footstool. Where then is a house you could build for Me? And where is a place that I may rest?"

Isaiah 66:1

The temple was the earthly place that God established for worship, so that people could fellowship together in praise of our Creator. However, true worship begins in our hearts. Jesus Christ is not only our Creator, but He is the head of the Church and the world is His footstool.

Privileged

This is eternal life, that they may know You, the only true God, and Jesus Christ whom You have sent.
John 17:3

Have you ever unwittingly overheard an intimate conversation? Well, that's exactly what this chapter of John is like. We are privileged to overhear Jesus as He speaks to the Father. His prayer includes concern for those whom the Father has given to Him. He prayed that God's power would keep us from being swayed by the world and the evil one.

Trust in God's Strength

About this time tomorrow I will send you a man from the land of Benjamin, and you shall anoint him to be prince over My people Israel; and he will deliver My people from the hand of the Philistines. For I have regarded My people, because their cry has come to Me.

1 Samuel 9:16

Lord, help me trust in Your strength to instill, infuse, and instruct so that I serve You obediently.

Special Service

Now the word of the LORD came to me saying,
"Before I formed you in the womb I knew you,
and before you were born I consecrated you;
I have appointed you a prophet to the nations."

Jeremiah 1:4–5

Lord, I pray for answers to the dilemmas that
plague our society. Not knowing whom You have
called for special service, let me respect and revere
each life with hope, anticipation, and gratitude.

Abide in Truth

*When Jesus had spoken these words,
He went forth with His disciples over the ravine
of the Kidron, where there was a garden, in which
He entered with His disciples. Now Judas also,
who was betraying Him, knew the place.*
John 18:1–2

What could possibly be worse than being betrayed?
Having the one who is disloyal rise up from among
those who called you friend! Lord, make straight
my wavering path! Help me abide in Your truth.

Power and Authority

Fill your horn with oil, and go;
I will send you to Jesse the Bethlehemite,
for I have selected a king for Myself
among his sons.
1 Samuel 16:1

Saul had been summoned by the Lord for service as king. Yet Saul had relied on his own strength and it failed him. This character flaw eventually brought him down to complete disgrace, and the Lord chose another king. Lord, keep me from misusing the power and authority You give me.

A Way Through

"They will fight against you, but they will not overcome you, for I am with you to deliver you," declares the LORD.

Jeremiah 1:19

We humans are resilient, able to withstand almost any hardship as long as we know we're not abandoned. God always provides a way through, for Israel and for us.

Your Message, Lord

*Jesus answered him, "I have spoken openly
to the world; I always taught in synagogues,
and in the temple, where all the Jews come together;
and I spoke nothing in secret. Why do you question
Me? Question those who have heard what I spoke
to them; they know what I said."*

John 18:20–21

Lord, break down my walls of stubbornness that
prevent me from hearing, seeing, and rallying to
Your message.

Power

Then David spoke to the men who were standing by him, saying, ". . .Who is this uncircumcised Philistine, that he should taunt the armies of the living God?"

1 Samuel 17:26

David refused to allow Goliath's attitude to stand unchallenged. His victory came by the power of the Lord, not by man's might. Lord, remind me of this when I face my own "giants."

True Peace

"At that time they shall call Jerusalem 'The Throne of the LORD,' and all the nations will be gathered to it, to Jerusalem, for the name of the LORD; nor will they walk anymore after the stubbornness of their evil heart."

Jeremiah 3:17

True peace will reign in Israel when Christ returns again to earth (Matthew 24:29–39). Lord, help me wait!

Stand Firm

Pilate also wrote an inscription and put it on the cross.
It was written, "Jesus the Nazarene,
the King of the Jews."
John 19:19

God overruled the Jews' request when Pilate
refused to change the sign on the cross. Pilate
knew Christ was exactly who He claimed to be,
King of the Jews, the promised Messiah. Yet Pilate
lacked the gumption to stand by his conviction.
Lord, give me the courage to stand firmly in my
convictions.

Let God Take Charge

"The LORD therefore be judge and decide between
you and me; and may He see and plead my cause,
and deliver me from your hand."

1 Samuel 24:15

Saul had pursued David relentlessly. David and his
men came upon Saul as he slept. David, instead of
killing Saul, cut off a small corner of his robe as a
gesture of respect for God's anointed. Despite his
circumstances and discomfort, David would allow
the Lord charge over this matter.

The Central Focus

Their Redeemer is strong, the LORD of hosts is His
name; He will vigorously plead their case
so that He may bring rest to the earth.

Jeremiah 50:34

Israel looked forward in time to redemption by the
Messiah, while we take a view back in time to the
cross on which our Redeemer died. Christ then
becomes the central focus for both the Old and
New Testaments.

King of the Jews

Pilate then took Jesus and scourged Him. And the soldiers twisted together a crown of thorns and put it on His head, and put a purple robe on Him; and they began to come up to Him and say, "Hail, King of the Jews!" and to give Him slaps in the face.

John 19:1–3

Lord, in my behalf You withstood extreme torture. Am I adding new but invisible wounds each time I refuse to crown You King of my own life?

Unforgettable Friend

Now the Philistines were fighting against Israel, and the men of Israel fled from before the Philistines and fell slain on Mount Gilboa. The Philistines overtook Saul and his sons; and the Philistines killed Jonathan and Abinadab and Malchi-shua the sons of Saul.

1 Samuel 31:1–2

Who has faithfully stood beside you through life's triumphs and tragedies? For David this person was Jonathan. Father, help me to be a faithful, loving, and unforgettable friend.

In Spirit and in Truth

The LORD is in His holy temple.
Let all the earth be silent before Him.
Habakkuk 2:20

Lord, instill in my heart a reverence for Your
house. May I worship You in Spirit and in truth.

The Miracle

Now on the first day of the week Mary Magdalene
came early to the tomb, while it was still dark, and saw
the stone already taken away from the tomb. So she
ran and came to Simon Peter and to the other disciple
whom Jesus loved.

John 20:1–2

Peter and John ran to the tomb and then left
again—too soon, missing the miracle. "But Mary
was standing outside the tomb weeping. . . . She
turned around and saw Jesus standing there" (John
20:11,14).

Turn to God

*The people have fled from the battle,
and also many of the people have fallen and are dead;
and Saul and Jonathan his son are dead also.*

2 Samuel 1:4

David refused to gloat over Saul's death. He poured forth his personal anguish by writing a song for Saul and Jonathan (2 Samuel 1). David turned to God for guidance, and God gave him a fresh call to leadership.

A Vision of Hope

The word of the LORD came expressly to Ezekiel
the priest. . .in the land of the Chaldeans. . .
and there the hand of the LORD came upon him.

Ezekiel 1:3

Ezekiel had been groomed for the priesthood, but
that was forever altered when he was taken captive.
But in captivity, the Lord called him to prophesy
concerning Israel's coming restoration and the
temple. Lord, despite my own problems and
challenges I can keep going forward as long as You
show me a vision of hope.

Accountable

*And when He had spoken this, He said to him,
"Follow Me!" Peter, turning around, saw the disciple
whom Jesus loved following them. . . . So Peter seeing
him said to Jesus, "LORD, and what about this man?"
Jesus said to him, "If I want him to remain until I come,
what is that to you? You follow Me!"*

John 21:19–22

Lord, in this special encounter You call me to be
accountable for my own walk with you. Please
enable me!

Unity among Believers

*And David brought up his men who were with him,
each with his household. . . . Then the men
of Judah came and there anointed David
king over the house of Judah.*
2 Samuel 2:3–4

Lord, I know that You appointed David as king of
Israel, uniting Your chosen people who were then
divided. May I submit my own life to You that You
might use me to create unity among believers.

Depend on God's Word

*Then He said to me, "Son of man, go to the house
of Israel and speak with My words to them."*
Ezekiel 3:4

How did you become a Christian? By hearing
the Word of God? That's the way I came to know
Him as Savior. At times we are unwilling to risk
presenting the gospel message because of personal
rejection. However, the outcome isn't our problem,
it's God's. Lord, help me depend on Your Word to
accomplish all You intend.

His Spirit

John baptized with water, but you will be baptized
with the Holy Spirit not many days from now.

Acts 1:5

The disciples had learned how to live out the
Christian life from observing Jesus Christ during
His three years of ministry. Now they would watch
Christ ascend to heaven; no longer would they
speak to Him face-to-face. However, Jesus sent
them His Spirit, that they might have God's power
within them as His Church began.

God's Will

The king said to Nathan the prophet,
" . . . The ark of God dwells within tent curtains."
Nathan said to the king, "Go, do all that is in
your mind, for the LORD is with you."
2 Samuel 7:2–3

Nathan the prophet supplied David with a
quick agreement to his plan to build the temple.
However, when Nathan inquired of the Lord, he
learned that God had chosen David's son to build
the temple. Lord, help me discern Your will.

Understanding the Word

*Then the Spirit lifted me up, and I heard
a great rumbling sound behind me,
"Blessed be the glory of the LORD in His place."*
Ezekiel 3:12

Ezekiel's vision can be compared to one that John,
the writer of the Gospel of John and the Book of
Revelation, described. Lord, I'm so grateful that
You have intricately woven Your Word for me.
Thank You that Your very Spirit enables me to
understand these difficult passages.

Filled with the Holy Spirit

*When the day of Pentecost had come,
they were all together in one place.
And suddenly there came from heaven a noise like
a violent, rushing wind, and it filled the whole house
where they were sitting. And they were all filled with
the Holy Spirit and began to speak with other tongues,
as the Spirit was giving them utterance.*

Acts 2:1–2, 4

I honor Your Holy Spirit, not only for insight into
Your Word, but for the power to obey You.

Help Me Be Accountable, Lord

*So David sent and inquired about the woman.
And one said, "Is this not Bathsheba,
the daughter of Eliam, the wife of Uriah the Hittite?"
David sent messengers and took her,
and when she came to him, he lay with her. . . .
The woman conceived.*

2 Samuel 11:3–5

David knew Bathsheba was Uriah's wife but he seduced her anyway. An even greater sin occurred as David tried to cover his tracks. Lord, help me to be accountable to You.

Until the End of Time

"So as I live," declares the Lord GOD, "surely,
because you have defiled My sanctuary with all your
detestable idols and with all your abominations,
therefore I will also withdraw, and My eye will
have no pity and I will not spare."

Ezekiel 5:11

God always preserves a remnant of His people.
And it will be so until the end of time on this
earth.

Fresh Boldness

*Having been exalted to the right hand of God,
and having received. . .the promise of the Holy Spirit,
He has poured forth this which you both see and hear.
Therefore let all the house of Israel know for certain
that God has made Him both Lord and Christ—
this Jesus whom you crucified.*

Acts 2:33, 36

A fresh new boldness filled the disciples. Jesus
Christ had become the bridge between the Old
and New Testaments. Everything in their history
had pointed to this moment. Lord, strengthen my
faith.

Keep Your Eyes on God

Because by this deed you have given occasion to the enemies of the LORD to blaspheme, the child also that is born to you shall surely die.

2 Samuel 12:14

The stillborn death of our first child was a devastating blow to my husband and me. As I read this passage of David's suffering, my heart could readily identify with the pain he endured. Gracious Lord, help me look to You for my own help.

A Message of Peace

So My hand will be against the prophets who see false visions. . . . It is definitely because they have misled My people by saying, "Peace!" when there is no peace.

Ezekiel 13:9–10

People today get sick of hearing doomsday forecasters. Those living in Ezekiel's day reacted the same way. They preferred a message of peace rather than hearing of the need for repentance. Lord, help me to share Your truth even in the midst of an apathetic and, yes, hostile world.

Savior

Then Peter, filled with the Holy Spirit, said to them,
". . .By the name of Jesus Christ. . .whom you crucified,
whom God raised from the dead—by this name this
man stands here before you in good health. . . .
And there is salvation in no one else; for there is no
other name under heaven that has been given among
men by which we must be saved."

Acts 4:8, 10, 12

What a dynamic change in Peter! To know Christ
as Savior is too great a joy to be contained!

A Picture of Peace

*"The LORD is my rock and my fortress and my deliverer;
my God, my rock, in whom I take refuge;
my shield and the horn of my salvation,
my stronghold and my refuge; my savior."*
2 Samuel 22:2–3

David's understanding of his Lord, using this
concept of refuge, is a picture of the peace,
comfort, and security we seek for our lives. I praise
You only, Jesus, my Rock of faith and redeemer.

Walk Daily with God

The king talked with them, and out of them all not one was found like Daniel, Hananiah, Mishael and Azariah; so they entered the king's personal service. As for every matter of wisdom and understanding about which the king consulted them, he found them ten times better than all the magicians and conjurers who were in all his realm.

Daniel 1:19–20

Lord, help me to walk with You that Your will might be accomplished on earth.

A Way to Salvation

*Peter said to them, "Repent, and each of you be baptized
in the name of Jesus Christ for the forgiveness of your
sins; and you will receive the gift of the Holy Spirit."*

Acts 2:38

Lord, I thank You that those who lived before
Jesus came to earth were given the same gospel
message through the prophets. I thank You that
You have always provided a way to salvation.

Accept God's Will

As David's time to die drew near, he charged Solomon his son, saying, ". . .Keep the charge of the LORD your God, to walk in His ways, to keep His statutes, His commandments, His ordinances, and His testimonies, according to what is written in the Law of Moses."

1 Kings 2:1, 3

One of David's sons, Adonijah, wanted the throne. He planned a full challenge to Solomon's leadership and it cost him his life. Lord, please help me to graciously accept Your will and be satisfied.

From Harm

Then Nebuchadnezzar. . .said, "Look!
I see four men loosed and walking about in the midst
of the fire without harm, and the appearance of
the fourth is like a son of the gods!"
Daniel 3:24–25

Jesus was with Daniel's friends in the fire. Lord,
be my faithful God, just as You were to Daniel's
friends. Keep me from harm as I walk through the
fires in my own life.

Enduring Messages of Truth

*The priests and the captain of the temple guard and
the Sadducees came up to them, being greatly disturbed
because they were teaching the people and proclaiming
in Jesus the resurrection from the dead. And they laid
hands on them and put them in jail.*

Acts 4:1–3

Both Jesus and John the Baptist had been killed
for preaching the truth. Even as Peter and John
now spoke, they were arrested. Was their message
wasted? Not at all. There will always be a remnant
who hears and responds.

An Understanding Heart

So give Your servant an understanding heart to judge
Your people to discern between good and evil. For who
is able to judge this great people of Yours?

1 Kings 3:9

Lord, how I pray that such wisdom would be given
to lawmakers. I also need Your guidance for my
family. Help me remember to turn to You in my
dilemmas.

Abiding Love

When he had come near the den to Daniel, he cried out with a troubled voice. The king spoke and said to Daniel, "Daniel, servant of the living God, has your God, whom you constantly serve, been able to deliver you from the lions?" Then Daniel spoke to the king, "O king, live forever! My God sent His angel and shut the lions' mouths."

Daniel 6:20–22

Lord, I praise You that the next morning, the king found evidence of Your abiding love.

Thank You for Change, Lord

*Saul was in hearty agreement with putting him to
death. And on that day a great persecution began
against the church in Jerusalem; and they were all
scattered throughout the regions of Judea and Samaria,
except the apostles.*

Acts 8:1

Thank You, God, for changing Saul into Paul!

A Flair for the Dramatic

Elisha said, "Please, let a double portion of your spirit be upon me." He said, "You have asked a hard thing. Nevertheless, if you see me when I am taken from you, it shall be so for you. . . ." As they were going along and talking, behold, there appeared a chariot of fire and horses of fire which separated the two of them. And Elijah went up by a whirlwind to heaven. Elisha saw it.

2 Kings 2:9–12

Elisha had received God's Spirit. I love God's flair for the dramatic!

Keep Me from Deception, Father

*"Behold, a fourth beast, dreadful and terrifying
and extremely strong; and it had large iron teeth.
It devoured and crushed and trampled down the
remainder with its feet; and it was different from
all the beasts that were before it."*

Daniel 7:7

God made Daniel the recipient of but some of the
pieces of this prophetic puzzle. Lord, I know from
Your Word that this last terrible beast will be the
antichrist. Do not let me be deceived by him.

Willing to Serve

Now about that time Herod the king laid hands on some who belonged to the church in order to mistreat them. And he had James the brother of John put to death with a sword.
Acts 12:1–2

His heart filled with grief for a martyred brother, John must have contemplated his promise of commitment and then gone on with his ministry. Lord, I know that although James paid the ultimate price, he now worships before Your heavenly throne. Help me serve You as well.

In His Presence

*They forsook all the commandments of the LORD their
God and made for themselves molten images. . . .
Then they. . .sold themselves to do evil in the sight
of the LORD, provoking Him. So the LORD was very
angry with Israel and removed them from His sight.*

2 Kings 17:16–18

Lord, what things keep me from Your presence?
Please bring me back into true worship that I
might not be led astray.

The Second Coming

From the issuing of a decree to restore and rebuild Jerusalem until Messiah the Prince there will be seven weeks and sixty-two weeks; it will be built again, with plaza and moat, even in times of distress. Then after the sixty-two weeks the Messiah will be cut off and have nothing, and the people of the prince who is to come will destroy the city and the sanctuary.

Daniel 9:25–26

Jesus, I await Your second coming and the eventual demise of the evil one.

How I Might Serve

*And he found a Jew named Aquila. . .with his wife
Priscilla. . . . He came to them, and because he was
of the same trade, he stayed with them and they were
working; for by trade they were tent-makers.*

Acts 18:2–3

Paul worked as a tentmaker so that he might
support his travels within his ministry. Lord, show
me today how I might serve You and present the
gospel message to others.

In His Will

Then David said to Ornan, "Give me the site of this threshing floor, that I may build on it an altar to the LORD; for the full price you shall give it to me, that the plague may be restrained from the people."

1 Chronicles 21:22

Directly following an incident of King David's disobedience to the Lord that brought a siege of pestilence on the land, God commanded David to obtain a property for the temple. Lord, let me not test Your patience!

Angels

Then he said to me, "Do not be afraid, Daniel, for from the first day that you set your heart on understanding this and on humbling yourself before your God, your words were heard, and I have come in response to your words. Now I have come to give you an understanding of what will happen to your people in the latter days, for the vision pertains to the days yet future."

Daniel 10:12, 14

Lord, let Your angels protect and enlighten me to truth.

Source of Life

Paul, a bond-servant of Christ Jesus, called as an apostle, set apart for the gospel of God. . .concerning His Son, who was born of a descendant of David according to the flesh, who was declared the Son of God with power by the resurrection from the dead. . . through whom we have received grace and apostleship.

Romans 1:1–5

Paul had come to know the true source of life. And with this knowledge came a mission for the rest of his days on earth.

In Your Heart

Solomon amassed chariots and horsemen.
He had 1,400 chariots and 12,000 horsemen,
and he stationed them in the chariot cities
and with the king at Jerusalem.

2 Chronicles 1:14

Long before Israel even had a king, the Lord had established certain standards for this monarch. He was not to multiply horses for himself, nor cause the people to return to Egypt to get horses (Deuteronomy 17:14–16). God didn't want the king's heart to turn away from following Him.

The Powerful Word

*In his place a despicable person will arise,
on whom the honor of kingship has not been conferred,
but he will come in a time of tranquility
and seize the kingdom by intrigue.*

Daniel 11:21

The antichrist is a real person who will one day
deviously slither onto the scene. He will appear
indispensable at a time of worldwide, unsolvable
chaos. Lord, compel me with a new urgency to
study Your powerful Word, that I might bring it to
others.

Obey God's Word

Do you suppose. . .when you pass judgment on those
who practice such things and do the same yourself,
that you will escape the judgment of God?

Romans 2:3

Those who know little about the Word of
God seem to parade about this verse. Paul was
addressing hypocrites who "know the ordinance
of God," yet practice things which are "worthy of
death" (Romans 1:32). But people recite this verse
to those who have the audacity to suggest they obey
God's Word. They try to silence the truth.

Abide Completely

*Hezekiah became king when he was twenty-five
years old. . . . He did right in the sight of the LORD,
according to all that his father David had done. In the
first year of his reign, in the first month, he opened the
doors of the house of the LORD and repaired them.*

2 Chronicles 29:1–3

Lord, help me learn to abide in You completely.

The Book of Life

Now at that time Michael, the great prince who stands guard over the sons of your people, will arise. And there will be a time of distress such as never occurred since there was a nation until that time; and at that time your people, everyone who is found written in the book, will be rescued.

Daniel 12:1

Lamb of God, who takes away sin, I want to know my name is written in Your book!

Always There

*For if Abraham was justified by works, he has
something to boast about; but not before God.
For what does the Scripture say? "Abraham believed
God, and it was credited to him as righteousness."*

Romans 4:2–3

I thank You that I worship a God whose Word can
be trusted. I know Jesus will always be there for me.

God's Word Will Come to Pass

Now in the first year of Cyrus king of Persia, in order to fulfill the word of the LORD by the mouth of Jeremiah, the LORD stirred up the spirit of Cyrus king of Persia, so that he sent a proclamation throughout all his kingdom.

Ezra 1:1

Approximately 175 years before King Cyrus was even born, God had spoken through the prophet Isaiah concerning him (Isaiah 44:24, 28). Lord, I am absolutely sure that what You have said will come to pass.

A Unique Invitation

*When the L*ORD *first spoke through Hosea, the L*ORD *said to Hosea, "Go, take to yourself a wife of harlotry and have children of harlotry; for the land commits flagrant harlotry, forsaking the L*ORD.*"*

Hosea 1:2

The Book of Hosea reveals the brokenness of God's own heart as He watched Israel wander away. "And I will say to those who were not My people, 'You are My people!'" (Hosea 2:23). Lord, thank You for Your unique invitation.

True and Lasting Peace

Therefore, having been justified by faith, we have peace with God through our Lord Jesus Christ, through whom also we have obtained our introduction by faith into this grace in which we stand; and we exult in hope of the glory of God.

Romans 5:1–2

People have scoured every nook and cranny of the globe in search of peace. But every new road eventually leads to the dead end of dissatisfaction. The only true and lasting peace comes from Jesus Christ.

God's Way

*Now when the enemies of Judah and Benjamin
heard that the people of the exile were building a
temple to the LORD God of Israel. . .then the people
of the land discouraged the people of Judah,
and frightened them from building.*

Ezra 4:1, 4

Lord, You always cause the wicked to stumble.
Thank You!

A Clean Slate

Return to the LORD. Say to Him, "Take away all iniquity and receive us graciously, that we may present the fruit of our lips." I will heal their apostasy, I will love them freely, for My anger has turned away from them.

Hosea 14:2, 4

Our holy God is not obligated to forgive us. Yet what hope would we have for change if God didn't wipe the slate of our past failures clean and provide us with the strength to start afresh?

A Child of God

*Therefore there is now no condemnation
for those who are in Christ Jesus. For the law
of the Spirit of life in Christ Jesus has set you
free from the law of sin and of death.*

Romans 8:1–2

I rejoice that I am a child of God and heir to the
kingdom! Hallelujah!

Always Done

A decree has been issued by me. . .and it has been discovered that that city has risen up against the kings in past days, that rebellion and revolt have been perpetrated in it, that mighty kings have ruled over Jerusalem. . .and that tribute, custom and toll were paid to them.

Ezra 4:19–20

I read that shortly after King Darius issued his decree, work began again to finish the temple. Lord, Your will is always done!

Rejoice!

*What the gnawing locust has left, the swarming locust
has eaten; and what the swarming locust has left, the
creeping locust has eaten; and what the creeping locust
has left, the stripping locust has eaten.*

Joel 1:4

The information contained in the book of Joel is
referred to as eschatology, or a study of the end
times, and parallels other passages in scripture.
When Jesus spoke to His disciples, He too quoted
this prophetic passage. Lord, I rejoice in Your
Word.

Yield in Faith

*Brethren, my heart's desire and my prayer
to God for them is for their salvation.*

Romans 10:1

Is the deepest concern of your heart that those
whom you love will share heaven with Christ?
Lord, clarify Your Word, that women may yield in
faith.

Never Lose Sight

*They said to me, "The remnant there in the province
who survived the captivity are in great distress and
reproach, and the wall of Jerusalem is broken down
and its gates are burned with fire." When I heard these
words, I sat down and wept and mourned for days; and
I was fasting and praying before the God of heaven.*

Nehemiah 1:3–4

Lord, let me learn from Nehemiah's example.
Let me seek Your will through prayer and study,
never losing sight of Your Son.

Fair and Just

Hasten and come, all you surrounding nations,
and gather yourselves there. Bring down,
O LORD, Your mighty ones.

Joel 3:11

Jerusalem will be the site of the world's last and
greatest battle as the surrounding nations rage
against the Holy City. The almighty God of the
universe will intervene on Israel's behalf. Lord,
I don't like to consider the brutality of this final
judgment. However, I know that You are fair and
just and have given men and women ample time
and warning to repent.

Effective Weapon

*Therefore I urge you. . .to present your bodies a living
and holy sacrifice, acceptable to God, which is your
spiritual service of worship. And do not be conformed
to this world, but be transformed by the renewing
of your mind.*

Romans 12:1–2

The weapons God provides for us are spiritual.
We must become proficient with such an arsenal
before it can be effective. So, if the Lord says His
Word is a weapon, we've got to read it, know it, and
follow it.

Rely on God's Strength

*And all the people gathered as one man at the square. . .
and they asked Ezra the scribe to bring the book of the
law of Moses. . . . Then Ezra the priest brought the law
before the assembly of men, women and all who could
listen with understanding.*

Nehemiah 8:1–2

Through inspired teamwork, Nehemiah and the
remnant of Israel finished rebuilding the wall in
only fifty-two days. Nehemiah led the people and
relied on God's strength. Lord, let Nehemiah be an
example for me.

Walk in Obedience

*Thus says the LORD, "For three transgressions
of Damascus and for four I will not revoke its
punishment. . . . I will also. . .cut off the inhabitant
from the valley of Aven. . . . So the people of
Aram will go exiled to Kir."*

Amos 1:3, 5

Throughout the Old Testament we've read
accounts of God's wrath directed toward those
whom He loved who were flagrantly disobedient.
But God also extended His loving hand of
protection to those who walked in obedience.

Dedicated Life

I commend to you our sister Phoebe. . .that you receive
her in the LORD in a manner worthy of the saints,
and that you help her in whatever matter she may
have need of you; for she herself has also been a
helper of many, and of myself as well.

Romans 16:1–2

Paul viewed dedicated people as living testimonies
to all that God's Spirit could accomplish in one's
character. Lord, as a woman, let my life, like
Phoebe's, shine before others.

Thank You for Forgiveness

*On the seventh day, when the heart of the king was
merry with wine, he commanded. . .the seven eunuchs
who served in the presence of King Ahasuerus, to bring
Queen Vashti before the king with her royal crown
in order to display her beauty. . . . But Queen Vashti
refused to come at the king's command.*
Esther 1:10–12

Thank You, Lord God, King of all kings, that You
forgive me when I fail to come into Your presence.

The Head of the Church

"Then the house of Jacob will be a fire and the house of Joseph a flame; but the house of Esau will be as stubble. And they will set them on fire and consume them, so that there will be no survivor of the house of Esau," for the LORD has spoken.

Obadiah 1:18

Lord, let me remember that it is Christ who is the head of His Church and I am but a member of the Body.

Disciples

To those who have been sanctified in Christ Jesus,
saints by calling, with all who in every place call on the
name of our Lord Jesus Christ, their Lord and ours.

1 Corinthians 1:2

These Corinthians, whom Paul address as saints,
were far from model citizens, but he wasn't
ashamed to call them brothers. Lord, am I truly
Your disciple?

Available and Obedient

Then the king's attendants, who served him, said,
"Let beautiful young virgins be sought for the king. . . .
Then let the young lady who pleases the king be queen
in place of Vashti." And the matter pleased the king,
and he did accordingly.

Esther 2:2–4

In the beginning, Esther was unaware of how God
would use her life. Lord, let me be as available and
obedient to You.

Yield Your Life

"Arise, go to Nineveh the great city, and cry against it,
for their wickedness has come up before Me."
But Jonah rose up to flee to Tarshish from
the presence of the LORD.
Jonah 1:2–3

God had solicited Jonah's help in bringing a
message to Nineveh. However, Jonah's fear of these
Ninevites loomed far greater than his fear of the
Lord. Finally Jonah responded in faith. Lord,
please help me yield in the areas You're ready to
work on in my life.

True Understanding

For to us God revealed them through the Spirit; for the
Spirit searches all things, even the depths of God. . . .
Now we have received. . .the Spirit who is from God,
so that we may know the things freely given to us by God.

1 Corinthians 2:10, 12

Here's an excuse heard often: "We can't try to interpret
the Bible ourselves because we'll get confused." But
to refuse the Holy Spirit the opportunity to instruct
you, as He promised He would, is to refuse true
understanding.

God's Plan

In those days, while Mordecai was sitting at the king's gate, Bigthan and Teresh, two of the king's officials from those who guarded the door, became angry and sought to lay hands on King Ahasuerus. But the plot became known to Mordecai and he told Queen Esther, and Esther informed the king in Mordecai's name.

Esther 2:21–22

Lord, what a dark hour this was for Your people, but You had already put a plan into action.

Creative Solutions

*So they picked up Jonah, threw him into the sea, and
the sea stopped its raging. And the LORD appointed
a great fish to swallow Jonah, and Jonah was in the
stomach of the fish three days and three nights.*

Jonah 1:15, 17

Lord, You alone have the ability to deliver a great
fish to swallow a man whole and not harm him.
Help me trust You for creative solutions to all my
problems.

A Temple of God

*Do you not know that you are a temple of God
and that the Spirit of God dwells in you? If any man
destroys the temple of God, God will destroy him,
for the temple of God is holy, and that is what you are.*
1 Corinthians 3:16–17

Lord, let me live as though I believe You are permeating my very being. Amen.

Praise God!

Then the king's scribes were summoned on the thirteenth day of the first month, and it was written just as Haman commanded to the king's satraps. . . . Letters were sent by couriers to all the king's provinces to destroy, to kill and to annihilate all the Jews.

Esther 3:12–13

Mordecai replied, "Who knows whether you have not attained royalty for such a time as this?" (Esther 4:14). Esther trusted God. I praise Him!

Our Cries

"I called out of my distress to the LORD, and He answered me. I cried for help from the depth of Sheol; You heard my voice." Then the LORD commanded the fish, and it vomited Jonah up onto the dry land.

Jonah 2:2, 10

Now the Lord issued to Jonah a fresh call to go to Nineveh, that he might get the response right this time.

Held Accountable

Does any one of you, when he has a case against his neighbor, dare to go to law before the unrighteous and not before the saints? Do you not know that we will judge angels? How much more matters of this life?

1 Corinthians 6:1, 3

The verses above are meant to give you hope. The saints of God will one day judge those who operate within this world system of injustice. As God brings down justice, this world will be held accountable to Him.

Wisdom and Courage

So Esther replied, "My petition and my request is:
if I have found favor in the sight of the king,
and if it please the king to grant my petition
and do what I request, may the king and Haman
come to the banquet which I will prepare for them,
and tomorrow I will do as the king says."

Esther 5:7–8

Lord, thank You for giving Esther the wisdom and
courage to save her people and Your people, the Jews.

A God of Compassion

*When God saw their deeds, that they turned from their
wicked way, then God relented concerning the calamity
which He had declared He would bring upon them.
And He did not do it.*

Jonah 3:10

I praise my compassionate God!

Single. . .or Not?

It is good for a man not to touch a woman. But because
of immoralities, each man is to have his own wife,
and each woman is to have her own husband. . . .
But this I say by way of concession, not of command.
1 Corinthians 7:1–2, 6

If a woman can best serve God as part of a married couple, then the Lord will provide the mate she seeks. Single or married, show me how to make a difference, Lord.

Obedient, Loyal, and Trustworthy

*Then Esther spoke again to the king, fell at his feet,
wept and implored him to avert the evil scheme of
Haman the Agagite and his plot which he had devised
against the Jews. And the king extended
the golden scepter to Esther.*

Esther 8:3–4

Lord, I thank You for this account of Esther's
obedience, loyalty, and trust.

Lessons of Truth

Hear, O peoples, all of you; listen, O earth and all it contains, and let the Lord GOD be a witness against you, the Lord from His holy temple. For behold, the LORD is coming forth from His place. He will come down and tread on the high places of the earth.

Micah 1:2–3

Lord, keep me from following in the footsteps of the rebellious that I might not require bitter lessons of truth.

Prayers, Tithes, and Offerings

Who at any time serves as a soldier at his own expense? Who plants a vineyard and does not eat the fruit of it? Or who tends a flock and does not use the milk of the flock?

1 Corinthians 9:7

Paul chose to labor without receiving any wages so that no one could accuse him of presenting the gospel for personal gain. Lord, let me remember in my prayers, tithes, and offerings all those who labor to bring the Word of God to me and others.

Unwavering Faith

*There was a man. . .whose name was Job, and that
man was blameless, upright, fearing God and turning
away from evil. Seven sons and three daughters were
born to him. His possessions also were 7,000 sheep,
3,000 camels, 500 yoke of oxen, 500 female donkeys.*

Job 1:1–3

This, of course, was life as Job used to know it,
before his character was tested. His life became an
unwelcome ride on a trolley called tragedy. And
through all of this Job refused to blame God or to sin.

Guard My Mind

*Woe to those who scheme iniquity, who work out evil
on their beds! When morning comes, they do it,
for it is in the power of their hands.*

Micah 2:1

Lord, guard my mind from evil that I might not
ruminate on such things and be propelled into
ungodly actions. Instead, let me turn to Your Word,
which acts as a cleansing agent.

One Step Closer

*Now these things happened as examples for us,
so that we would not crave evil things as they also
craved. Nor let us act immorally, as some of them did,
and twenty-three thousand fell in one day.*

1 Corinthians 10:6, 8

By reading the entire Bible we have the privilege
of learning from God's dealings with men and
women throughout recorded history so we will
not fall into the same traps. Father, help me avoid
temptation by taking one step closer to You.

God Is So Good

Oh that my grief were actually weighed and laid in the
balances together with my calamity! For then it would
be heavier than the sand of the seas. . . . But it is still
my consolation, and I rejoice in unsparing pain, that I
have not denied the words of the Holy One.

Job 6:2–3, 10

Do we stand on the bedrock of knowledge about
God's goodness, despite the circumstances? Or do
we succumb to the opinions of friends?

Rejoice in His Coming

And He will arise and shepherd His flock in the strength of the LORD, in the majesty of the name of the LORD His God. And they will remain, because at that time He will be great to the ends of the earth. This One will be our peace.

Micah 5:4–5

I rejoice because Christ is coming back! "And on His robe and on His thigh He has a name written, 'King of kings, And Lord of lords' " (Revelation 19:16).

Blessed Assurance

Therefore I make known to you that no one speaking by the Spirit of God says, "Jesus is accursed"; and no one can say, "Jesus is Lord," except by the Holy Spirit.

1 Corinthians 12:3

Lord, I know if I'm listening to a message that makes me depressed and defeated, that's from Satan. I know the message that says I'm worth dying for is from Christ.

God Is in Control

"It is God who removes the mountains. . .who alone stretches out the heavens, and tramples down the waves of the sea; who makes the Bear, Orion and the Pleiades. . .who does great things, unfathomable, and wondrous works without number."
Job 9:5, 8–10

The God who has created all that we see, hear, touch, taste, and smell is able to control what we don't understand. Job recognized that both blessings and testing through trials flowed from the same loving hands.

The Price

What does the LORD require of you but to do justice,
to love kindness, and to walk humbly with your God?
Micah 6:8

Christ has already paid the price that needed to be exacted for our sins. The God of this universe became a man, and then He sacrificed His life so that we who could never deserve His mercy might obtain it. Jesus did all this because He is both just and kind.

Sweet Harmony

*If I speak with the tongues of men and of angels,
but do not have love, I have become a noisy gong
or a clanging cymbal.*

1 Corinthians 13:1

Even though we've prayed for godly mates, and
then relied on God's guidance, there will still be
times when our attempts to love are less than
perfect. However, if both man and woman turn
back to God's blueprint, harmony can be restored.

The Hand of the Lord

Speak to the earth, and let it teach you; and let the fish of the sea declare to you. Who among all these does not know that the hand of the LORD has done this, in whose hand is the life of every living thing, and the breath of all mankind?

Job 12:8–10

Lord, I know that even if I didn't have Your written Word, the order and perfection of Your creation still prove Your existence!

Meeting the Shepherd

And the earth will become desolate because of her inhabitants, on account of the fruit of their deeds. Shepherd Your people with Your scepter, the flock of Your possession which dwells by itself in the woodland, in the midst of a fruitful field. Let them feed in Bashan and Gilead as in the days of old.

Micah 7:13–14

I look forward to meeting my Shepherd!

Promise of a Savior

*But now Christ has been raised from the dead,
the first fruits of those who are asleep. For since by a
man came death, by a man also came the resurrection
of the dead. For as in Adam all die, so also in Christ
all will be made alive.*

1 Corinthians 15:20–22

From man's beginning in the Garden of Eden, one
Savior was promised (Genesis 3:15).

Turn to God

The Lord restored the fortunes of Job. . . . The Lord
blessed the latter days of Job more than his beginning;
and he had 14,000 sheep, and 6,000 camels,
and 1,000 yoke of oxen and 1,000 female donkeys.
And he had seven sons and three daughters.

Job 42:10, 12–13

Lord, through Job's pain, agony, and loss
You placed "wisdom in his innermost being"
concerning deep and marvelous truths about Your
character. When I am afflicted, remind me to turn
toward You.

Virtues

Behold, on the mountains the feet of him who brings good news, who announces peace! Celebrate your feasts, O Judah. . . . For never again will the wicked one pass through you; he is cut off completely.

Nahum 1:15

No news could be sweeter than the prophecy that a mighty enemy army was about to suffer a great demise. God gave Nahum just such a vision. Nahum then extolled the virtues of his God so that when God acted, the enemy would know exactly whom they had encountered.

Comfort

Blessed be the God and Father of our Lord Jesus Christ, the Father of mercies and God of all comfort; who comforts us in all our affliction so that we will be able to comfort those who are in any affliction with the comfort with which we ourselves are comforted by God.
2 Corinthians 1:3- 4

This is the purpose of our trials, that we might comfort one another and lean on the Lord's strength.

Christ's Account

If then you regard me a partner, accept him as you would me. But if he has wronged you in any way or owes you anything, charge that to my account.
Philemon 1:17–18

Father, thank You that my sins have been charged to Christ's account. Thank You that He paid the debt.

Firm Ground

But the righteous will live by his faith.
Habakkuk 2:4

In whom is our faith placed? If our faith is in
Christ, we are established upon firm ground.
But if it's in systems, programs, or even religion,
it's doomed to fail.

Momentum

I know a man in Christ who fourteen years ago. . .was caught up into Paradise and heard inexpressible words, which a man is not permitted to speak. On behalf of such a man will I boast; but on my own behalf I will not boast, except in regard to my weaknesses.

2 Corinthians 12:2, 4–5

Lord, Your magnificent presence is all I need to provide me with the momentum to continue spreading Your Word.

The Messiah

God, after He spoke long ago to the fathers in the
prophets. . .in these last days has spoken to us in
His Son. . . . When He had made purification of sins,
He sat down at the right hand of the Majesty on high.
Hebrews 1:1–3

The book of Hebrews confirmed to those who had
left the rituals of Judaism that they still had a high
priest who could petition the Father for them. He is
Jesus Christ, their Messiah, our Savior and Lord.

Evidence of Faith

Then it will come about on the day of the LORD's sacrifice that I will punish the princes, the king's sons and all who clothe themselves with foreign garments.

Zephaniah 1:8

Zephaniah's call from the Lord involved dislodging those who were indifferent to God. The latest opinion polls show that a majority of us in America claim to believe in God. But how is faith evidenced? As surely as judgment fell upon Israel for their sins, it will ultimately fall on us.

The Gospel of Grace

*I am amazed that you are so quickly deserting Him
who called you by the grace of Christ, for a different
gospel. . .there are some who are disturbing you and
want to distort the gospel of Christ.*

Galatians 1:6–7

Jewish believers were transitioning from the Law,
filled with regulations, and beginning to follow
the gospel of grace. A group began wooing them
back to the old legalism. Therefore, Paul left on
journeys to bring the gospel of grace to those who
were being seduced by this group.

A Heavenly Calling

Therefore, holy brethren, partakers of a heavenly calling, consider Jesus, the Apostle and High Priest of our confession; He was faithful to Him who appointed Him, as Moses also was in all His house. For He has been counted worthy of more glory than Moses, by just so much as the builder of the house has more honor than the house.

Hebrews 3:1–3

The opportunity to follow Christ lies before me. Lord, help me respond.

Seek Him

*Seek the LORD, all you humble of the earth
who have carried out His ordinances;
seek righteousness, seek humility. Perhaps you
will be hidden in the day of the LORD's anger.*

Zephaniah 2:3

Thank You, Father, that prayer can place me in
Your presence.

Christ's Call

For am I now seeking the favor of men, or of God?
Or am I striving to please men? If I were still trying to
please men, I would not be a bond-servant of Christ.
Galatians 1:10

Paul didn't sit around asking men for their
opinions. Christ's call was sufficient. Therefore,
he devoted himself to study, prayer, and
meditation alone with his Lord. What are my own
misconceptions concerning Your Word, Lord?
Teach me the true meaning of the scriptures.

Free in Christ

*For it is written that Abraham had two sons,
one by the bondwoman and one by the free woman.*

Galatians 4:22

Paul uses these two sons to illustrate the status
of the unbeliever versus her changed relationship
once she commits her life to Christ. Once we were
slaves to sin, but with our redemption in Christ we
have become free.

To Fulfillment

"Thus says the LORD of hosts, 'This people says, "The time has not come, even the time for the house of the LORD to be rebuilt."'" Then the word of the LORD came by Haggai. . .saying, "Is it time for you yourselves to dwell in your paneled houses while this house lies desolate?" Now therefore, thus says the LORD of hosts, "Consider your ways!"

Haggai 1:2–5

Lord, whatever task is overwhelming me today, You have the strength to see it through to fulfillment.

The Good News

*Let us fear if, while a promise remains of entering His
rest, any. . .may seem to have come short of it. For
indeed we have had good news preached to us, just as
they also; but the word they heard did not profit them,
because it was not united by faith in those who heard.*

Hebrews 4:1–2

Dear God, You have kept Your part of the bargain,
in obtaining salvation for me. Whether I respond
to this salvation is up to me.

King of Peace

For this Melchizedek, king of Salem, priest of the Most
High God. . .was first of all, by the translation of his
name, king of righteousness, and then also. . .king of
peace. Without father, without mother, without genealogy,
having neither beginning of days nor end of life, but made
like the Son of God, he remains a priest perpetually.

Hebrews 7:1–3

Melchizedek's priesthood is a perpetual one. The
Levitical priesthood, no longer necessary after
Christ's death on the cross, ended when the temple
was destroyed.

God Stands Watch

*I saw at night, and behold, a man was riding on a red
horse. . . . Then I said, "My lord, what are these?". . .
And the man who was standing among the myrtle trees
answered and said, "These are those whom the LORD
has sent to patrol the earth."*
Zechariah 1:8–10

Zechariah's name means "God remembers." And
the message he received from the Lord came at a
time when Israel most needed to be reminded that
their God still stood watch over them.

God's Gifts

*But the fruit of the Spirit is love, joy, peace, patience,
kindness, goodness, faithfulness, gentleness,
self-control; against such things there is no law.*
Galatians 5:22–23

Why is God showering us with these gifts? Because
they prove that He can enter a human life and
affect her or him with change, that others might
also be won to Christ as they observe this miracle.

Consider It All Joy

James, a bond-servant of God and of the Lord Jesus Christ, to the twelve tribes who are dispersed abroad: Greetings. Consider it all joy, my brethren, when you encounter various trials, knowing that the testing of your faith produces endurance.

James 1:1–3

How grateful I am, Lord, that You're not willing that any should perish, especially those of Your own family.

Day 310

Unlimited Power

*"Jerusalem will be inhabited without walls because
of the multitude of men and cattle within it. For I,"
declares the LORD, "will be a wall of fire around her,
and I will be the glory in her midst."*

Zechariah 2:4–5

At a time when only a remnant of Israel had
returned to Jerusalem, the Lord is promising that
at a future time they will become a great nation.
How grateful I am, Lord, to know that Your might
and unlimited power protect Israel.

A Sense of Belonging

Blessed be the God and Father of our Lord Jesus Christ, who has blessed us with every spiritual blessing in the heavenly places in Christ, just as He chose us in Him before the foundation of the world, that we should be holy and blameless before Him.

Ephesians 1:3–4

Lord, help me and each woman reading this to enjoy the safety, protection, and sense of belonging that come from being chosen.

The Friend of God

You see that faith was working with his works, and as a result of the works, faith was perfected; and the Scripture was fulfilled which says, "And Abraham believed God, and it was reckoned to him as righteousness," and he was called the friend of God.

James 2:22–23

Abraham's faith was evident by his actions. No matter what God required of him, Abraham obeyed God. Therefore, all of his actions were born out of the call God had on his life.

True Holiness

The LORD will possess Judah as His portion
in the holy land, and will again choose Jerusalem.
Be silent, all flesh, before the LORD;
for He is aroused from His holy habitation.
Zechariah 2:12–13

True holiness cannot reign within Israel until
the Messiah, Jesus Christ, comes to inhabit this
nation. Jesus will finally reign as Israel's true King.

Sealed by the Holy Spirit

*In Him, you also. . .were sealed in Him with the Holy
Spirit of promise, who is given as a pledge
of our inheritance.*
Ephesians 1:13–14

Sealing waxes and metal impressions were used in
the past as both a security measure and a statement
of authenticity. The king's signet ring was pressed
into hot melted wax, leaving an indelible and
unique impression. Paul was inspired to use this
image to describe how we, as believers, are sealed
by God's Holy Spirit.

Infinite Wisdom

So also the tongue is a small part of the body, and yet it boasts of great things. See how great a forest is set aflame by such a small fire! And the tongue is a fire.

James 3:5–6

We all have difficulty either saying too much or not saying it right. Thank You, Jesus, for Your words of infinite wisdom.

Path to the Cross

Now Joshua was clothed with filthy garments and standing before the angel. He spoke and said to those who were standing before him, saying, "Remove the filthy garments from him." Again he said to him, "See, I have taken your iniquity away from you and will clothe you with festal robes."

Zechariah 3:3–4

God has provided the means for our atonement and will do all in His power to lead us to the foot of the cross that we might obtain it.

A Loving Partnership

*Wives, be subject to your own husbands, as to the
Lord. For the husband is the head of the wife,
as Christ also is the head of the church.*
Ephesians 5:22–23

Wives, our role is that of a helpmate, not a
doormat. It's critical to remember that God
intended marriage to be a partnership. Only the
Lord is capable of loving perfectly. So the next
time your marriage feels like a 90/10 proposition,
remember that He's giving 100 percent.

He Will Never Fail Us

According to the foreknowledge of God the Father, by the sanctifying work of the Spirit, to obey Jesus Christ and be sprinkled with His blood: May grace and peace be yours in the fullest measure.

1 Peter 1:2

Jesus Christ will never fail us. He alone possesses perfectly all the characteristics we most admire. For He remains faithful, just, loving, omnipotent, and eternal.

The Presence of God

And the angel of the LORD admonished Joshua, saying,
"Thus says the LORD of hosts, 'If you will walk in My
ways. . .then you will also govern My house and also
have charge of My courts, and I will grant you free
access among those who are standing here.'"
Zechariah 3:6–7

As incredible an offer as this might have been for
Joshua, an even more miraculous invitation awaits
those who accept Jesus as Savior. For immediately
they can enjoy the very presence of God.

True Source of Joy

*I thank my God in all my remembrance of you,
always offering prayer with joy in my every prayer for
you all, in view of your participation in the gospel from
the first day until now.*

Philippians 1:3–5

Paul was confined to prison when he wrote
this letter. His joy was not dependent upon
circumstances. Rather, it overflowed from the
content of his heart, where the true source of joy
resides, Jesus Christ.

Conviction of Souls

*In this you greatly rejoice, even though now for a little
while, if necessary, you have been distressed by various
trials, so that the proof of your faith, being more
precious than gold which is perishable, even though
tested by fire, may be found to result in praise and glory
and honor at the revelation of Jesus Christ.*

1 Peter 1:6–7

What degree of persecution are you willing to
endure that the gospel of truth might go forward
to a needy world? Thank You, Jesus, for convicting
my soul today.

The Rock

"For behold, the stone that I have set before Joshua;
on one stone are seven eyes. Behold, I will engrave an
inscription on it," declares the LORD of hosts, "and I will
remove the iniquity of that land in one day."
Zechariah 3:9

The rock which Zechariah describes here is Jesus
Christ, Israel's Messiah. Fulfilling Old Testament
prophecy, they rejected this cornerstone. Lord,
help me cherish the truth concerning the Messiah's
identity.

Encourage One Another

*Do nothing from selfishness or empty conceit, but with
humility of mind regard one another as more important
than yourselves; do not merely look out for your own
personal interests, but also for the interests of others.*
Philippians 2:3–4

As Christians we are called to encourage one
another in the faith. Paul, who spent so much of
his own life in prison, had a deep understanding
of the need for the reassurance and hope that the
Lord richly supplied.

Pass It On

*Therefore, putting aside all malice and all deceit and
hypocrisy and envy and all slander, like newborn babies,
long for the pure milk of the word, so that by it you
may grow in respect to salvation, if you have tasted the
kindness of the Lord.*

1 Peter 2:1–3

As mothers, grandmothers, stepmothers, and aunts,
we have a God-ordained call to teach children the
Word of God that they might someday enter the
kingdom of God.

A Natural Light

I see, and behold, a lampstand all of gold with its bowl
on the top of it, and its seven lamps on it with seven
spouts belonging to each of the lamps
which are on the top of it.
Zechariah 4:2

God's purpose for these visions was to motivate
Israel to rebuild the temple. The seven-branched
lampstand reminded Zechariah of the candelabra
that the Jews call the menorah. The menorah was
used in the temple as a natural light within the
holy place.

In Harmony

Therefore, my beloved brethren whom I long to see, my joy and crown, in this way stand firm in the Lord, my beloved. I urge Euodia and I urge Syntyche to live in harmony in the Lord.

Philippians 4:1–2

Lord, help me to remember that You surrendered all Your rights that I might know true freedom. Please show me how to persevere, make amends, and live in harmony.

By Example

*In the same way, you wives, be submissive to your own
husbands so that even if any of them are disobedient
to the word, they may be won without a word by the
behavior of their wives, as they observe your chaste and
respectful behavior.*

1 Peter 3:1–2

Lord, show me Your way through my difficulties.
If my spouse or boyfriend does not know You as
his Savior, help me lead by example.

Olive Branches

Then I said to him, "What are these two olive trees on the right of the lampstand and on its left?" Then he said, "These are the two anointed ones."

Zechariah 4:11, 14

While they are symbolically referred to as "olive branches," these are two men who spread the gospel to the Jews during the tribulation period. Lord, I pray that those in Israel will listen to the message of Your witnesses, that many might be saved.

Remain Strong

Praying always for you, since we heard of your faith in Christ Jesus. . .because of the hope laid up for you in heaven, of which you previously heard in the word of truth, the gospel, which has come to you.

Colossians 1:3–6

The culture of these people in Colosse was steeped in Oriental mysticism. They lived along the main trade route, which made for a variety of backgrounds and doctrines. Paul reaches out to this nucleus of believers that their foundation in Christ might remain strong.

Character Change

*His divine power has granted to us everything
pertaining to life and godliness, through the true
knowledge of Him who called us by His own glory
and excellence. For by these He has granted to us His
precious and magnificent promises, so that by them you
may become partakers of the divine nature.*

2 Peter 1:3–4

As we walk in step with Him, learning His ways,
we will eventually reflect these changes in our
character.

With Your Whole Heart

The word of the LORD of hosts came to me,
saying, "Say to all the people of the land and to the
priests, 'When you fasted and mourned in the fifth
and seventh months these seventy years, was it
actually for Me that you fasted?'"
Zechariah 7:4–5

God wanted His people to celebrate joyously with
a sense of gratitude to Him. Instead, the Israelites
had made nothing but rituals out of the holy days.
Lord, help me to love You with my whole heart.

The King of Kings

He is the image of the invisible God, the firstborn of all creation. For by Him all things were created, both in the heavens and on earth, visible and invisible, whether thrones or dominions or rulers or authorities—all things have been created through Him and for Him.

Colossians 1:15–16

Jesus Christ lived a sinless life and died on the cross of Calvary for my sins. I worship the King of kings!

A Loving God

By the word of God the heavens existed long ago
and the earth was formed out of water and by water,
through which the world at that time was destroyed,
being flooded with water.

2 Peter 3:5–6

How could a loving God destroy the very people
and their world that He created? Look at how much
time He provided for them to repent. From the time
Noah received the order to build the ark until the
rain began, a span of 120 years had elapsed.

God's Promise Has Come

"Behold, I am going to send My messenger, and he will clear the way before Me. And the Lord, whom you seek, will suddenly come to His temple; and the messenger of the covenant, in whom you delight, behold, He is coming," says the LORD of hosts.

Malachi 3:1

Jesus Christ, God's promise to the world, has come! Thank You for Your Word of Truth.

Revealed in Glory

When Christ, who is our life, is revealed, then you
also will be revealed with Him in glory. Therefore
consider the members of your earthly body as dead to
immorality, impurity, passion, evil desire, and greed,
which amounts to idolatry.

Colossians 3:4–5

Our churches are comprised of redeemed sinners.
Christ in us should cause a change in our lives.
It should make a visible difference in how we are
living our lives. For Christ has set up residence
within us.

The Reason

We have seen and testify and proclaim to you the eternal life, which was with the Father and was manifested to us.

1 John 1:2

Where will you find joy this Christmas? It's not in brightly colored packages under the tree. And unless your loved ones know the Lord, jubilation probably won't be present at your family gatherings either. Dear Lord, thank You for the knowledge that Jesus is still the "reason for the season."

The Revelation of Jesus

The Revelation of Jesus Christ, which God gave Him to show to His bond-servants, the things which must soon take place; and He sent and communicated it by His angel to His bond-servant John, who testified to the word of God and to the testimony of Jesus Christ, even to all that he saw.

Revelation 1:1–2

After God gave Malachi the prophecies concerning the Messiah's coming, He remained silent for over four hundred years. And then He spoke to us. . . through His blessed Son, Jesus Christ.

The True Peace

*There is no distinction between Greek and Jew,
circumcised and uncircumcised, barbarian, Scythian,
slave and freeman, but Christ is all, and in all.*

Colossians 3:11

To say we love Christ and yet maintain deeply
rooted prejudices against others is inconsistent
with everything He taught. Lord, let the true peace
of Christmas, which is Christ, be found in my
heart as I am obedient to Your command to love
others just as You have loved me.

Children of God

See how great a love the Father has bestowed on us,
that we should be called children of God; and such we
are. . . . Beloved, now we are children of God.
1 John 3:1–2

Lord, as I prepare to celebrate Your birth, the
greatest gift I can lay beside the manger is an act
of my will that makes me Your child. Yes, I have
been born again.

Break Down the Barriers

Behold, He is coming with the clouds, and every eye will see Him, even those who pierced Him; and all the tribes of the earth will mourn over Him. So it is to be. Amen.

Revelation 1:7

Father, when humans have failed me I tend to blame You for their choices. Please break down the barriers in my heart that I might worship Your Son this Christmas.

Spread the Gospel

*We give thanks to God always for all of you, making
mention of you in our prayers; constantly bearing
in mind your work of faith and labor of love and
steadfastness of hope in our Lord Jesus Christ in the
presence of our God and Father.*
1 Thessalonians 1:2–3

God meant for His Church to be dynamic. For
this is the place where His believers still gather
to worship and grow. Lord, help me to spread the
gospel to those yet unsaved around me.

Before the Father

The eyes of the LORD are toward the righteous
and His ears are open to their cry.
Psalm 34:15

The Spirit of God hears our cries and takes our
petitions before the Father who answers our
prayers, for we have confessed belief in Him.

The Fire in My Soul

But I have this against you,
that you have left your first love.

Revelation 2:4

There is nothing to compare with that "first bloom of love." This is the kind of love that God desires from us. That on-fire, totally consuming, single focus of our attention. O Lord, may Your Light be the fire in my soul!

Obedient Living

Therefore encourage one another, and build up one another. . . . Appreciate those who diligently labor among you, and have charge over you in the Lord and give you instruction. . .esteem them very highly in love because of their work. Live in peace with one another.

1 Thessalonians 5:11–13

God equates love with obedience. When Christ returns for His believers, we are to be found walking in His statutes. Lord, let me be found obediently living Your call and commission.

Loving Obedience

*Whoever believes that Jesus is the Christ
is born of God, and whoever loves the
Father loves the child born of Him.*

1 John 5:1

When our children disobey, we feel not only
extreme disappointment but a sense that they don't
love us. For if they did, they would understand that
our instructions are meant to guide them over the
rough terrain of life. This is exactly how God feels
when we fail to follow Him. For He equates love
with obedience.

A Rainbow

*Behold, a throne was standing in heaven,
and One sitting on the throne. And He who was sitting
was like a jasper stone and a sardius in appearance;
and there was a rainbow around the throne,
like an emerald in appearance.*
Revelation 4:2–3

This rainbow in heaven is not the half-bow we're
used to seeing. It is a complete circle because in
heaven all things are whole and finished. The most
amazing thing about this prism of color is that it
surrounds Christ.

Come Lord Jesus

*We request you, brethren, with regard to the coming
of our Lord Jesus Christ and our gathering together
to Him, that you not be quickly shaken from your
composure or be disturbed either by a spirit or a
message. . .to the effect that the day of the Lord has
come. Let no one in any way deceive you, for it will not
come unless the apostasy comes first, and the man of
lawlessness is revealed.*

2 Thessalonians 2:1–3

Even so, come Lord Jesus!

Adore Him!

Grace, mercy and peace will be with us, from God the Father and from Jesus Christ, the Son of the Father, in truth and love.

2 John 1:3

Jesus Christ. . .heralded by a star, proclaimed by angels, announced by the shepherds, and given by the Father to a world in need of a Savior. O, come let me adore Him!

God "in the Flesh"

And I saw in the right hand of Him who sat on the throne a book. . . . Then I began to weep greatly because no one was found worthy to open the book . . .and one of the elders said to me, "Stop weeping; behold, the Lion that is from the tribe of Judah. . .has overcome so as to open the book."

Revelation 5:1, 4 5

Lord, I can't truly celebrate Christmas unless I know that Jesus is God in the flesh, born to die for my sins.

Special Gifts

To Timothy, my true child in the faith: Grace, mercy and peace from God the Father and Christ Jesus our Lord. . . . The goal of our instruction is love from a pure heart and a good conscience and a sincere faith.

1 Timothy 1:2, 5

Paul wrote this letter to encourage Timothy in his own leadership role, knowing that the worst thing this young believer could do was to try and emulate Paul instead of Christ. Lord, show me how to use my special gifts.

True Identity

Anyone who. . .does not abide in the teaching of Christ, does not have God. . . . If anyone comes to you and does not bring this teaching, do not receive him into your house.

2 John 1:9–10

There is no greater evil than to fail to recognize who Jesus Christ is, God in the flesh. Today's scripture warns against false teachings. Lord, strengthen my faith so that I can love those who don't know You, so that I can reveal the true identity of Your Son.

Help Me Understand, Lord

I looked, and behold, a white horse, and he who sat on it had a bow; and a crown was given to him, and he went out conquering and to conquer. When He broke the second seal, I heard the second living creature saying, "Come." And another, a red horse, went out.

Revelation 6:2–4

Each of the four horsemen represents a different judgment that will come upon the earth. Lord, please help me understand Your Word.

Lift My Voice

*First of all, then, I urge that entreaties
and prayers, petitions and thanksgivings,
be made on behalf of all men.*

1 Timothy 2:1

Prayer is an act of worship on the part of the
created toward the Creator. It is simply talking to
God about everything that affects our lives. Spirit
of God, fall afresh on me that I might lift my voice
in petition to You.

Day 354

A Warm Reception

Beloved, you are acting faithfully in whatever you accomplish for the brethren, and especially when they are strangers; and they have testified to your love before the church. You will do well to send them on their way in a manner worthy of God.

3 John 1:5–6

Father, my church will likely be filled this Christmas with people who may only come once or twice a year. May I give these inquiring minds a warm reception.

Jesus Christ Holds the Keys

I looked, and behold, an ashen horse; and he who sat on it had the name Death; and Hades was following with him. Authority was given to them over a fourth of the earth, to kill with sword and with famine and with pestilence and by the wild beasts of the earth.

Revelation 6:8

In this vision, first came death and Hades followed him. Although death claims the body, and Hades the soul, only Jesus Christ holds the keys of death and Hades.

Special Recognition

*An overseer, then, must be above reproach, the husband
of one wife, temperate, prudent, respectable, hospitable,
able to teach, not addicted to wine or pugnacious,
but gentle, peaceable, free from the love of money.*

1 Timothy 3:2–3

Although this passage may appear directed toward
men, it applies to women as well. For the position
of deacon, referred to as a servant who assisted the
apostles, Paul singled out Phoebe, a deaconess, for
special recognition (Romans 16:1–2).

Hallelujah!

And I saw another angel ascending from the rising of the sun, having the seal of the living God; and he cried out with a loud voice to the four angels. . .saying, "Do not harm the earth or the sea or the trees until we have sealed the bond-servants of our God on their foreheads."
Revelation 7:2–3

Jesus Christ, the Alpha and Omega, is the King of kings and Lord of lords. And He's coming back! Hallelujah!

Use Me, Lord

I thank God. . .as I constantly remember you in my prayers night and day, longing to see you, even as I recall your tears, so that I may be filled with joy. For I am mindful of the sincere faith within you.
2 Timothy 1:3–5

Paul had to make sure that Timothy remained strong in the faith. For Timothy would now "carry the torch of faith" and continue bringing the gospel to all who would listen. Like Timothy, use me, Lord, to do Your will.

Set Time Aside

Beloved, while I was making every effort to write you about our common salvation, I felt the necessity to write to you appealing that you contend earnestly for the faith which was once for all handed down to the saints.

Jude 1:3

It's Christmas Eve and you probably have a busy day ahead. Has the luster of it worn off, replaced by the worldly pressures that overshadow Christ's birth? Jesus, remind me today to set aside time to be with You.

Joy Fills Our Hearts

While they were there, the days were completed for her to give birth. And she gave birth to her firstborn son; and she wrapped Him in cloths, and laid Him in a manger, because there was no room for them in the inn.

Luke 2:6–7

Joy fills our hearts as we celebrate Christmas. Thank You, Jesus, for willingly leaving heaven's throne to take on a human body and grow to manhood so You could die on the cross.

Pleasing God

Grace and peace from God the Father and Christ Jesus our Savior. For this reason I left you in Crete, that you would set in order what remains.

Titus 1:4–5

Lord, have I lived my life this year in a way that pleased You?

God Is Powerful

And I will grant authority to my two witnesses, and they
will prophesy for twelve hundred and sixty days, clothed
in sackcloth. These are the two olive trees and the two
lampstands that stand before the Lord of the earth.

Revelation 11:3–4

Lord, what a powerful God You are!

The Lamb of God

Let us rejoice and be glad and give the glory to Him,
for the marriage of the Lamb has come
and His bride has made herself ready.

Revelation 19:7

John the Baptist presented Jesus as the Lamb of God. Now John the Apostle reveals Christ again as the Lamb. This time He is preparing a supper in which His bride, "the Church," will be in the presence of the Lamb. This scene will take place in heaven, where the believers finally see Christ face-to-face.

Word of Truth

And I saw another angel. . .having an eternal gospel to preach to those who live on the earth. . .and he said with a loud voice, "Fear God, and give Him glory, because the hour of His judgment has come; worship Him who made the heaven and the earth and sea and springs of waters."

Revelation 14:6–7

Lord, while there is still time, please provide imaginative ways in which we can speak forth Your Word of Truth to all those whom we love.

The Song of Moses

And they sang the song of Moses, the bond-servant of God, and the song of the Lamb, saying, "Great and marvelous are Your works, O Lord God, the Almighty; righteous and true are Your ways, King of the nations!"

Revelation 15:3

Lord, You alone are worthy of our worship. I praise You with all my heart, and look forward to the day when I will worship You in heaven.

Notes